Advanced

Chinese Abacus

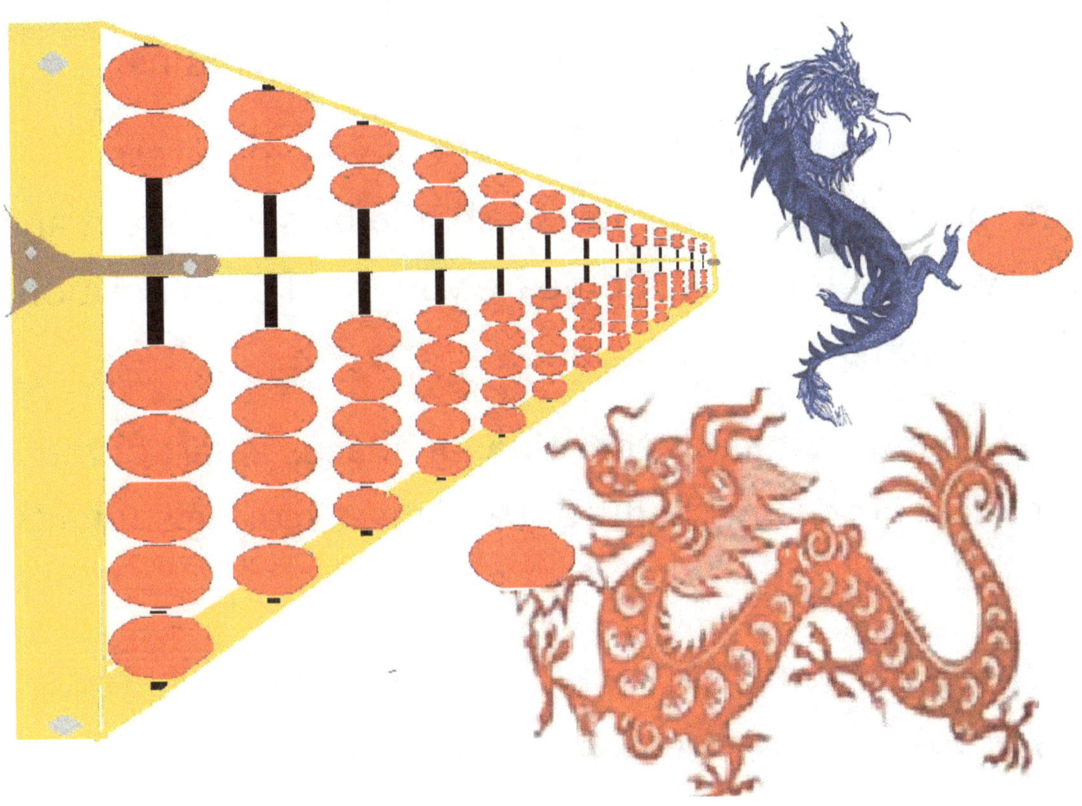

Joseph W. Salazar, J. D.

Public Accountant

This writing assumes that the reader has completed an introduction and basic course on abacus.

Advanced Chinese Abacus; working the same operations you did when learning the Chinese Abacus, but what is different is; the increased number of digits and the expected speed of completing the calculations. All calculating must be done on a Chinese Abacus (Suanpan) with at least twelve columns.

You may use a stop watch to keep track of your progress. Answers to problems on the abacus should be self evident and are not given in this course. Compare your final bead positions with the diagrams when in doubt.

I find that countries making the study of abacus a part of the mathematics curriculum produce the highest scoring students in the world.

Abacus trains the students of any age in concentration, focus, hand-eye coordination, anticipating needs, and visualization.

They are all good qualities for success in mathematics.

Abacus training will lead to mastery of mental-math; many students are able to use an imaginary abacus in calculations.

Check all answers manually or electronically to verify.

In addition and subtraction; keep the decimal points in Line

Such as   18.90   Not 18.9

          +24.07   +14.07

Time: 1 second per stroke

A   345 + 862 =   (12 seconds)

B   617 + 290=   (8 seconds)

C   389 + 1,204 =   (10 seconds)

D   1,804 +2,271 =   (9 seconds)

E   938,652 + 44,087 =   (15 seconds)

F	2,257	G	847	H	4,569
	3,891		3,279		2,008
	1,405		1,408		5,642
	6,402		22,990		5,040
	+ 994		+ 90,753		+ 6,573
	=		=		=
	(23 seconds)		(27 seconds)		(22 seconds)

Addition total time: 2.1 minutes to calculate, and 28 seconds to write down the sums; that is 2 minutes, 29 seconds to complete F through H.

Repeat the previous sums until you can make the time limit including writing down the sums after calculating each on the abacus.

These are financial calculations; each amount should have two decimal places, even if they are zeros.

I	$ 30,951.25	J	$29,804.13	K	$45,894.22
	34,618.50		414.73		89.36
	+ 14.28		+ 49,063.75		+28,069.33
	=$		=$		=$
	(00:00:20)		(00:00:24)		(00:00:24)

If you take more than 2 minutes for the last three; repeat until you can do them in 2minutes or less.

These are scientific types of calculations; anticipate at least 4 decimal places.

L   2.046 + 72.5 + 1,920.587 + 3.1416 =

M   0.5 + .03 + 100 + 22.5 =

N   20.06 +17.23 + 558 + 120 + 15.95 =

Complete in 47 seconds or less; then go on to next exercise.

O   Add each abacus to the next and graph your total.

        The decimal points are marked on the bar.

        Round to 4 decimal places

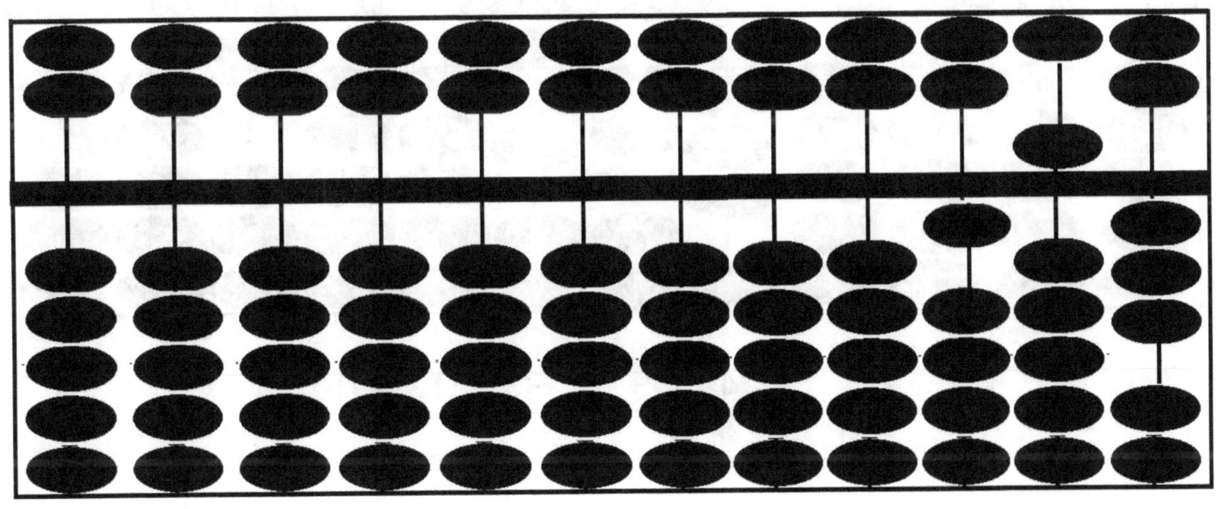

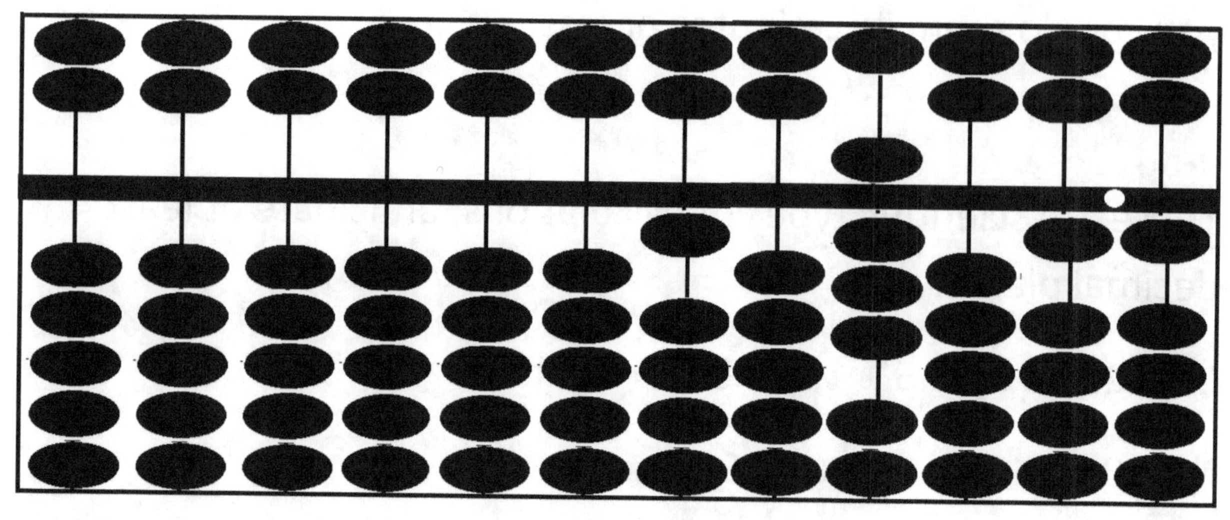

1 0 8 0 1 . 1

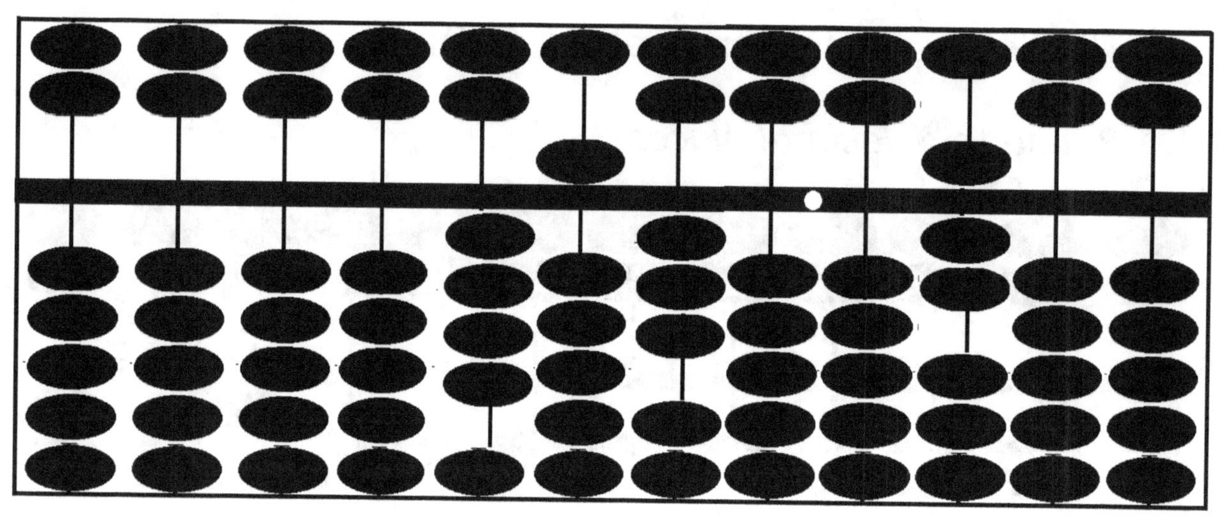

4 5 3 0 . 0 1 0 0

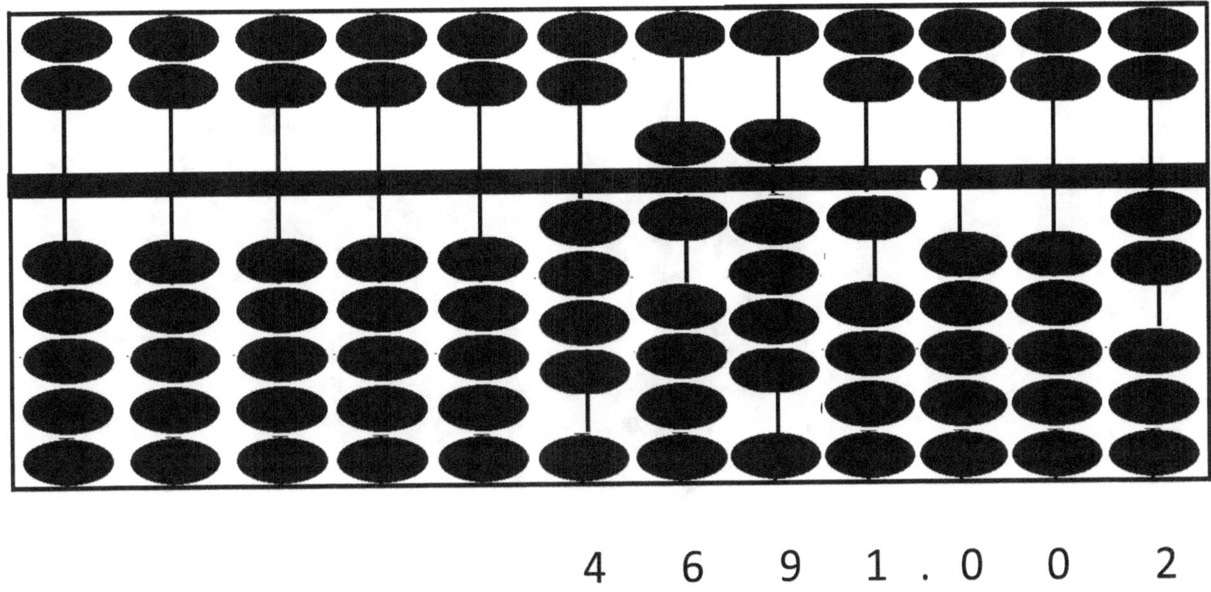

4   6   9   1 . 0   0   2

After adding the four preceding diagrams; fill in only the beads representing your final sum; just mark them with an X.

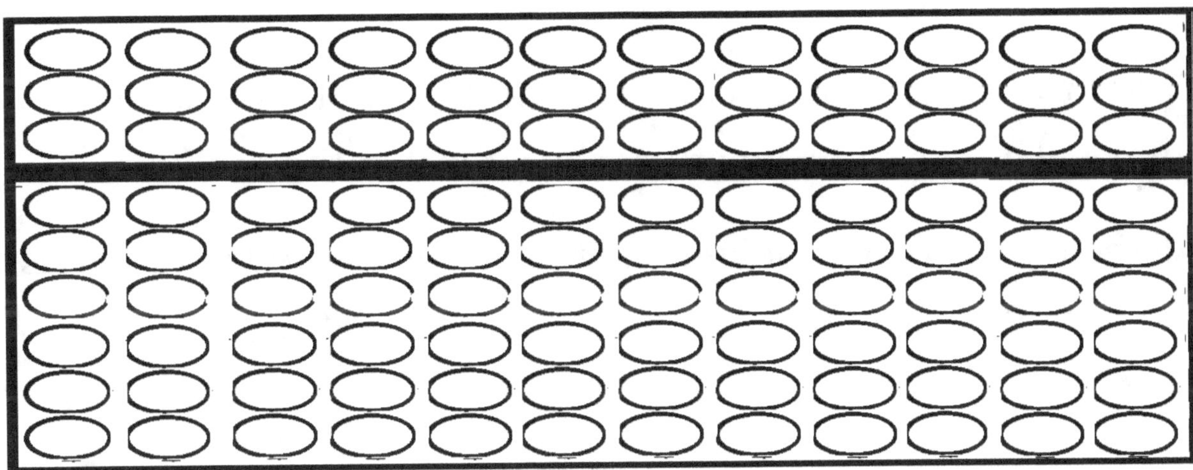

We have reviewed Addition; next we will review Subtraction.

These also may be larger numbers.

Count the digits of all the numbers in the problem assume the total will be the same length as the largest in the problem.

All the digits in the problem and the answer added together, is the number of seconds you have to find the difference.

A   592 − 237 =   B   845 − 364 =   C   1059 -915 =

D   35497 − 2211 =   E   6140 − 4927 = F   2718 -2048 =

G   645.83 -287.458 =   H   4.049 − 1.37 =

I   22.04 − 19.35 =   J   .0847 − 0.0032 =

Speed comes with practice

Subtract from or add to the abacus as indicated.

Draw in only the beads that represent your answers.

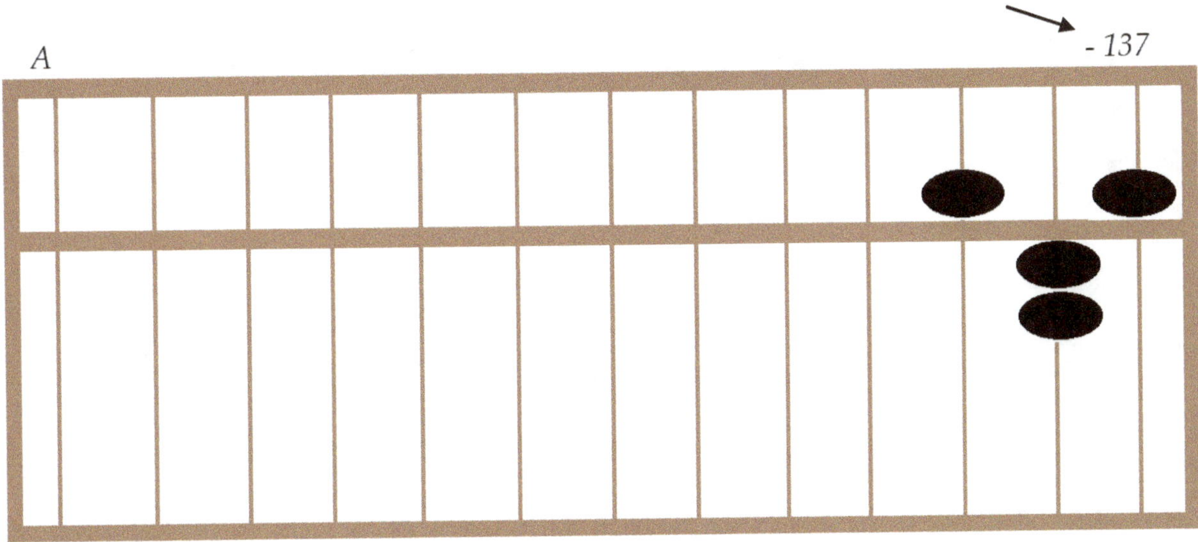

+ 19

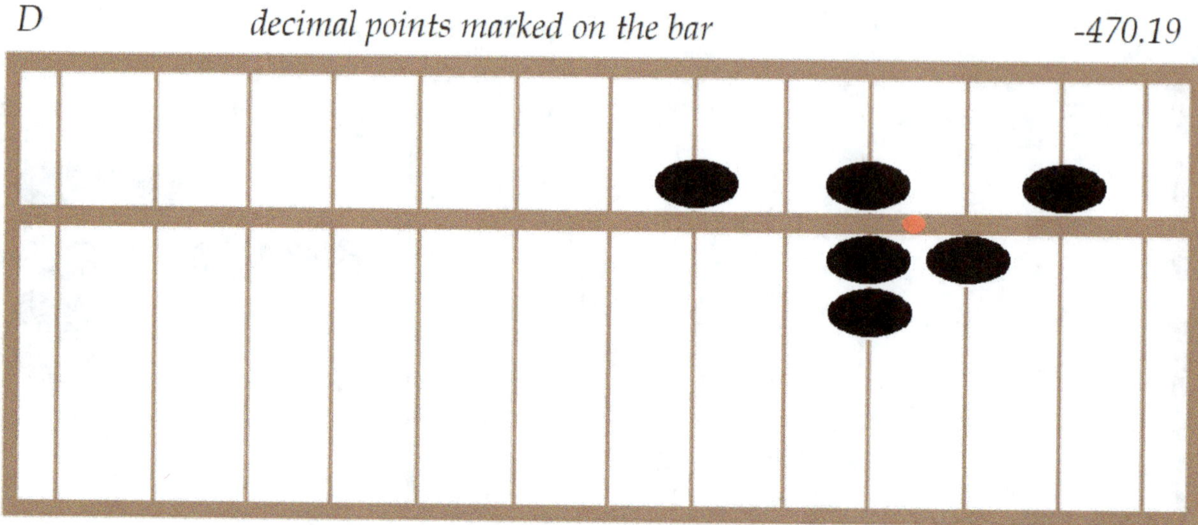

MIXED ADDITION & SUBTRACTION

A   375-291 +468.2 +307.46 +3399.1 − 14.05 =

B   28-5 +19 -6 +243 +1808 − 700 − 409 =

C	D	E	F
85,268	10,822	68,889	28,168
+39,109	+34,253	-56,197	+95,227
-16,732	+83,030	+66,571	+12,312
+30,928	-97,908	+41,919	-7,431
+69,399	+41,013	-67,530	+47,833
+92,975	-14,026	-14,071	-79,408
-31,373	+95,577	+66,012	+99,050
-52,391	+24,521	+51,511	+50,592
+77,610	-89,866	-22,051	-10,606
-50,889	+78,235	+68,997	+46,651
-8,365	-22,261	-7,064	-76,100
+40,365	+52,837	+59,352	-1,532
-10,872	+29,815	+17,928	+12,549
-10,277	-82,067	-63,932	-93,406
+35,104	+65,556	+8,511	+28,507
=	=	=	=

Finish each column faster than the last.

Let everyone present know you are on a clock and don't get distracted, if you do, then accept that you will have to try again. Keep a positive attitude.

Your answers: Draw only the beads representing your answers.

A

B

<u>C</u>

<u>D</u>

There are those who say "With the right hand, use the thumb to move beads up and the index finger to move beads down", but I think you need to use what is most efficient for you, to gain speed in abacus.

MULTIPLICATION

The rightmost digit of the product will have an initial base at the rightmost column, allowing for decimal places, if any; even if the digit is zero. The Product grows from right to left.

Set your multiplicand on the left and skip one or more columns then set the multiplier; finally, begin the product from the right.

When a multiplier digit is no longer needed, that digit may be removed and the column reclaimed as additional space for the product.

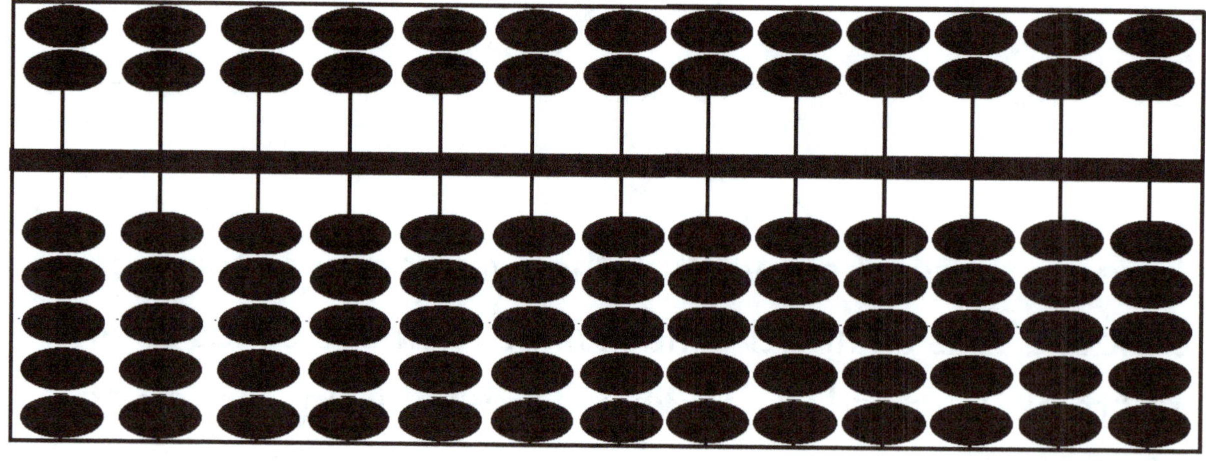

Multiplicand   Multiplier   Product

1 Digit Multiplier

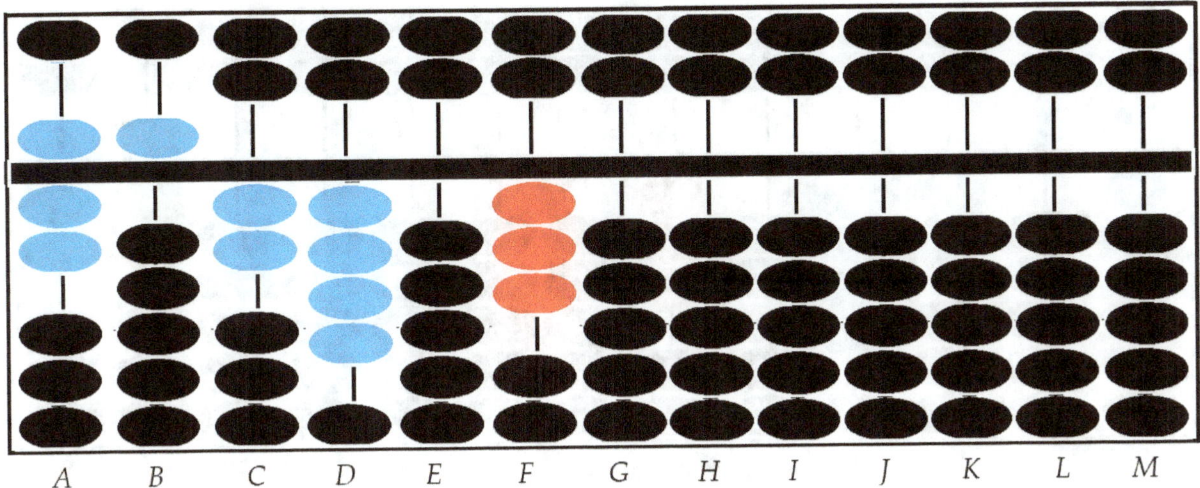

Multiply 7,524 by 3.

Multiplier 3 has an initial base at M, so from right to left the first digit of the product is at M.

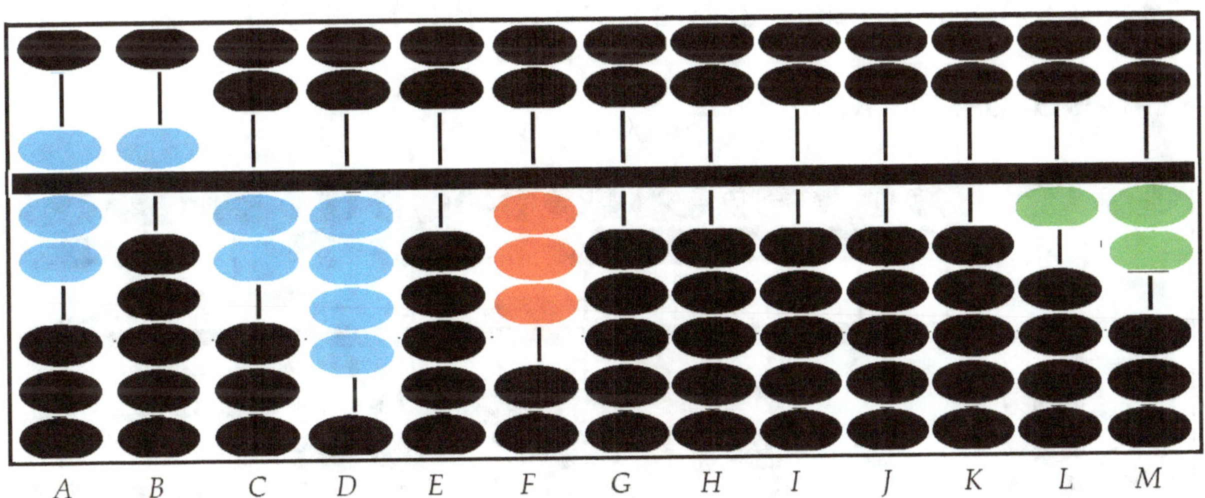

As we move to multiply 3 by 2 we move the base to L.

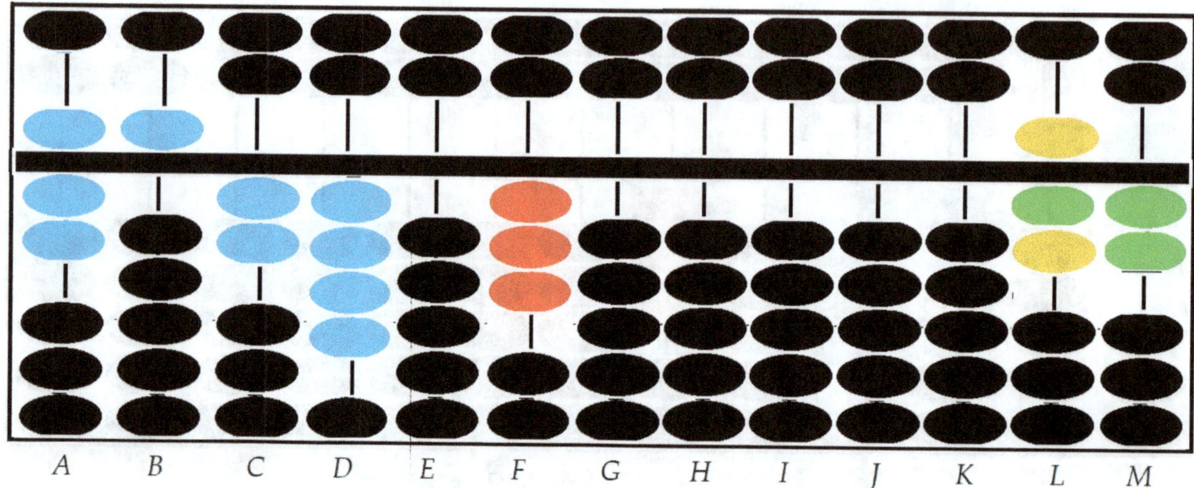

The fact that M spilled over to L does not change the base for multiplicand C.

One space to the left in the multiplicand means one space to the left in the product, so the base for B is K.

3 times 5; base is K.

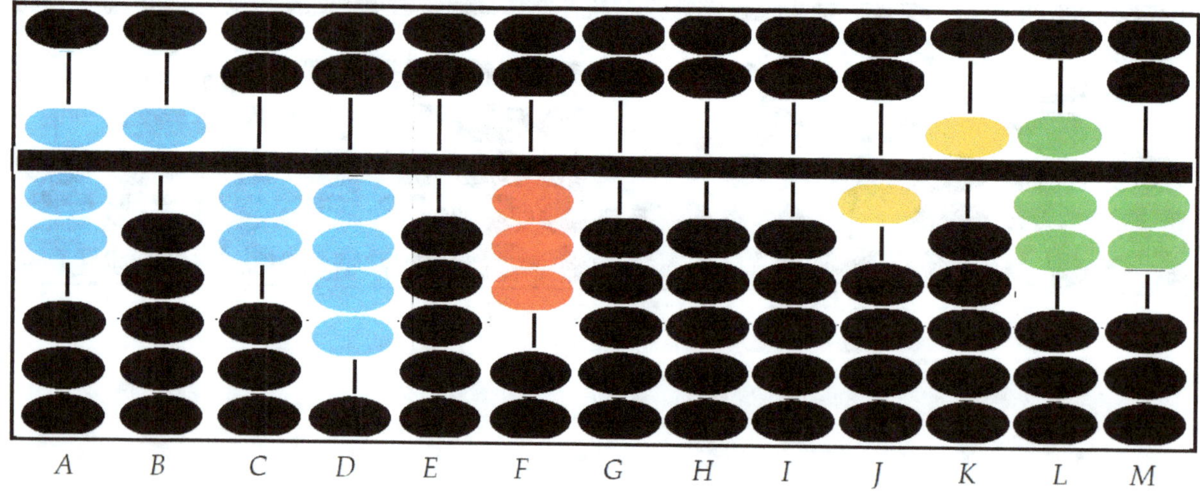

The initial base for A is J. 3 x 7

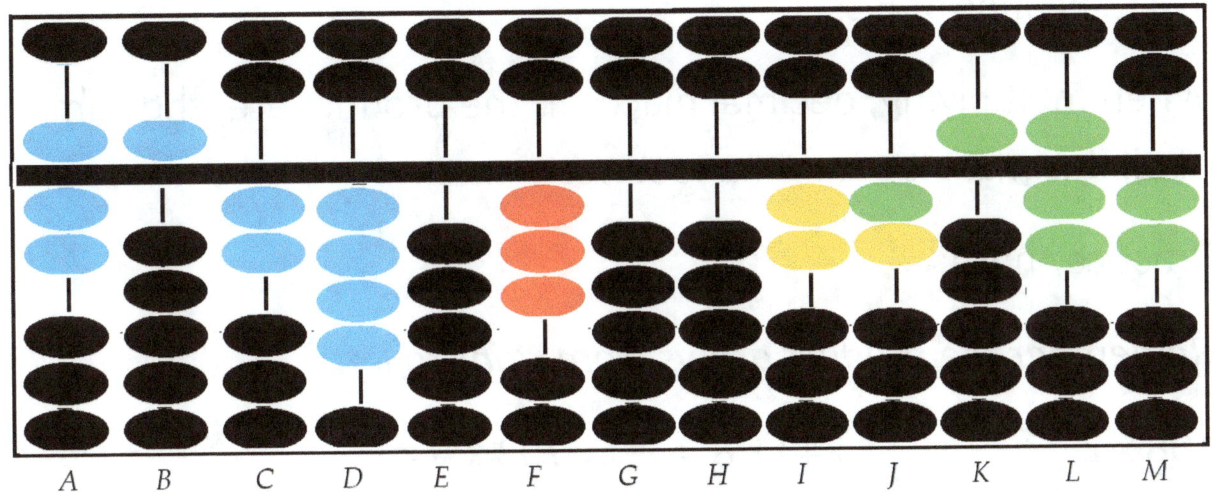

The product of 7,524 x 3 = 22,572

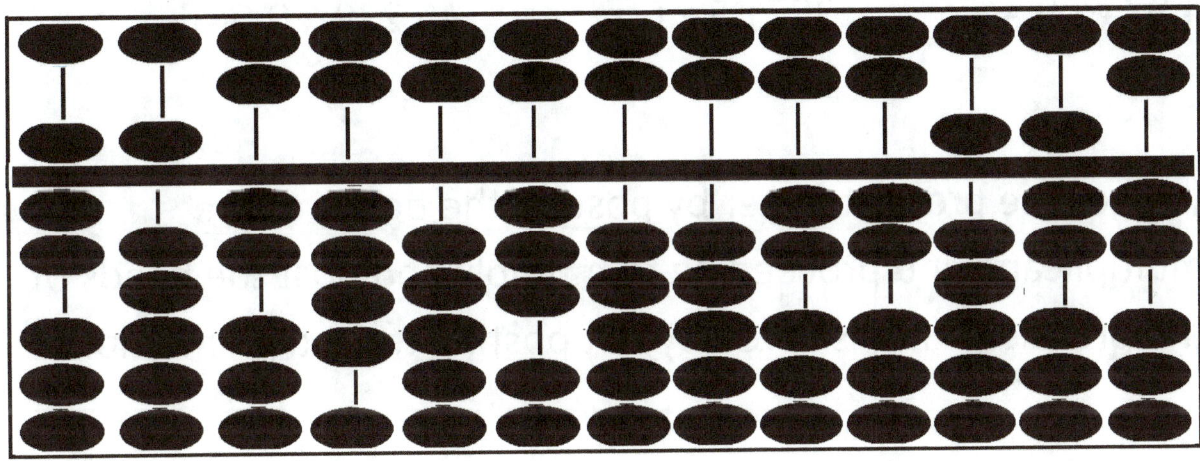

Time yourself on this operation. Start with all beads set to o.

129 x 9 =

How many seconds did you take to get the product?

If you used less than 12 seconds, you are really good!

If you used more than 15 seconds, try again until you can do it in 15 seconds or less.

When multiplying; decimal places in the product are, the sum of all decimal places in the factors.

Practice these:

Remember the product grows from right to left.

198 x 2 =   243 x 8 =   703 x 5 =

967 x 4 =   9,906.25 x 7 =   1.936 x 3 =

4.974 x 9 =   3871.5 x 6 =   46.239 x 0.6 =

We get the product faster by posting the beads of the multiplicand and proceeding to multiply and post the beads of the product. Time is saved by not posting the 1 digit multiplier.

Try the above again with this method; see how fast you have become in Abacus.

Complete these:

a

x 3

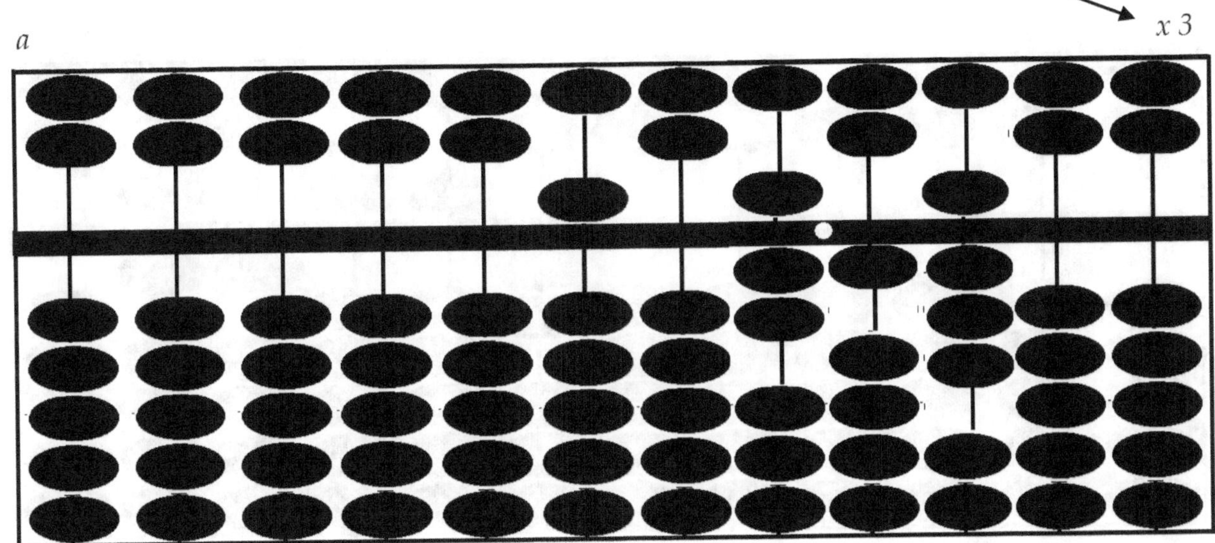

Mark only the beads representing your answers with **X**

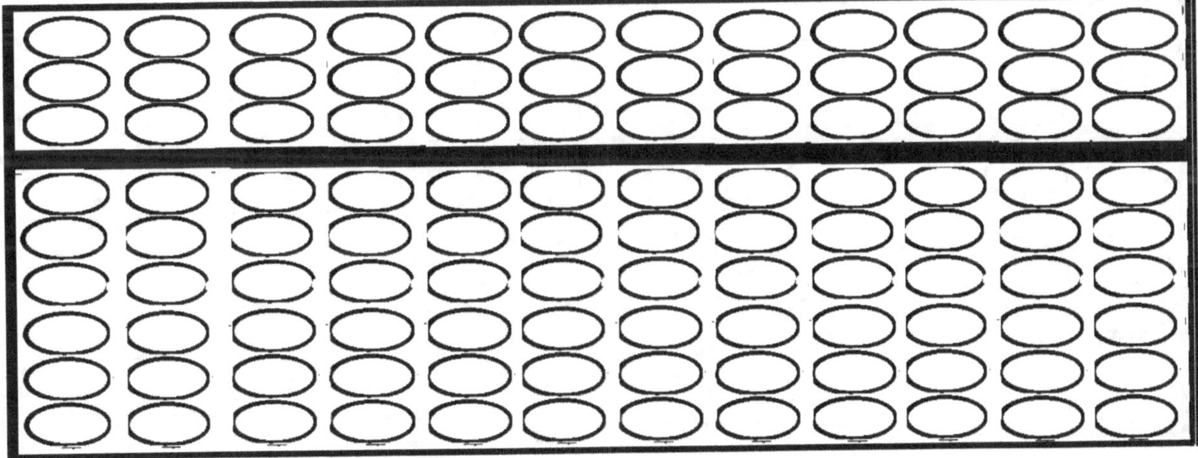

The decimal point is marked on the bar.

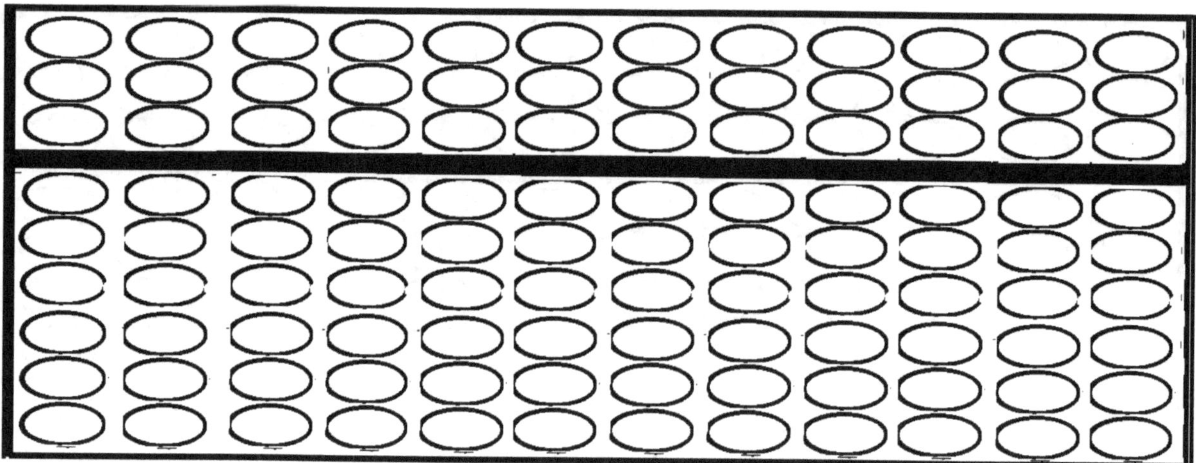

2 Digits Multiplier

The initial base, for the 2nd digit from the right multiplier, is the 2nd from the right column in the product.

The initial bases of digits in the product are the same as the place of the digits in the multiplier, right to left.

Multiply 7,524 by 35

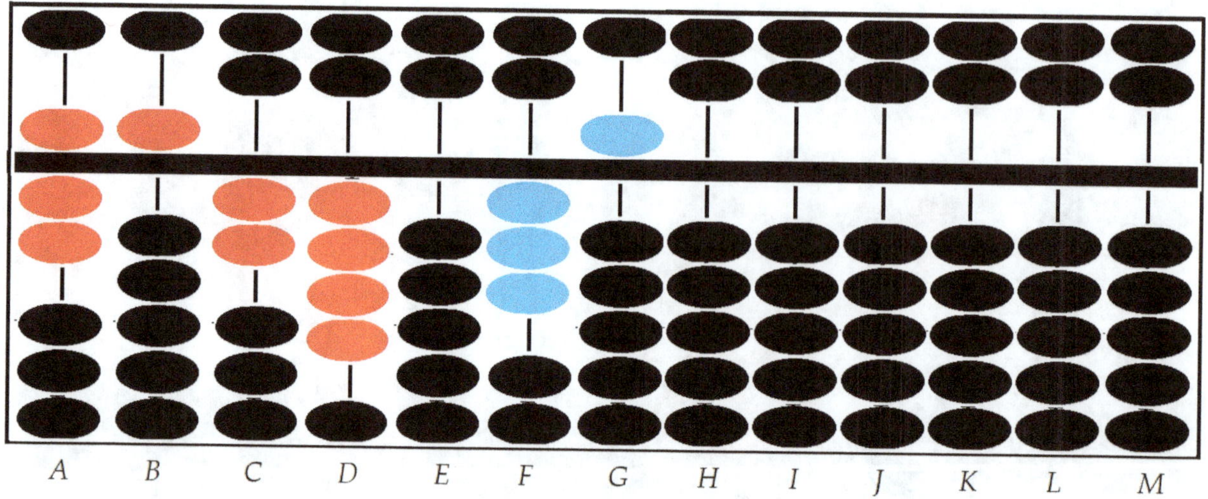

The initial base rule is the same as for the rightmost digit as it is for one digit.

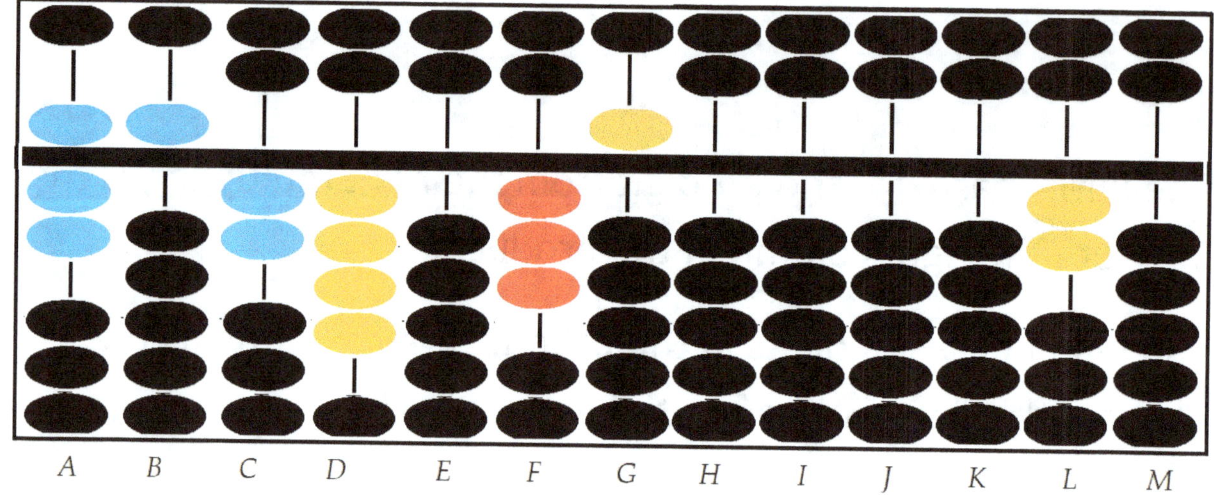

Remember the M column is a zero, but it is the base for D

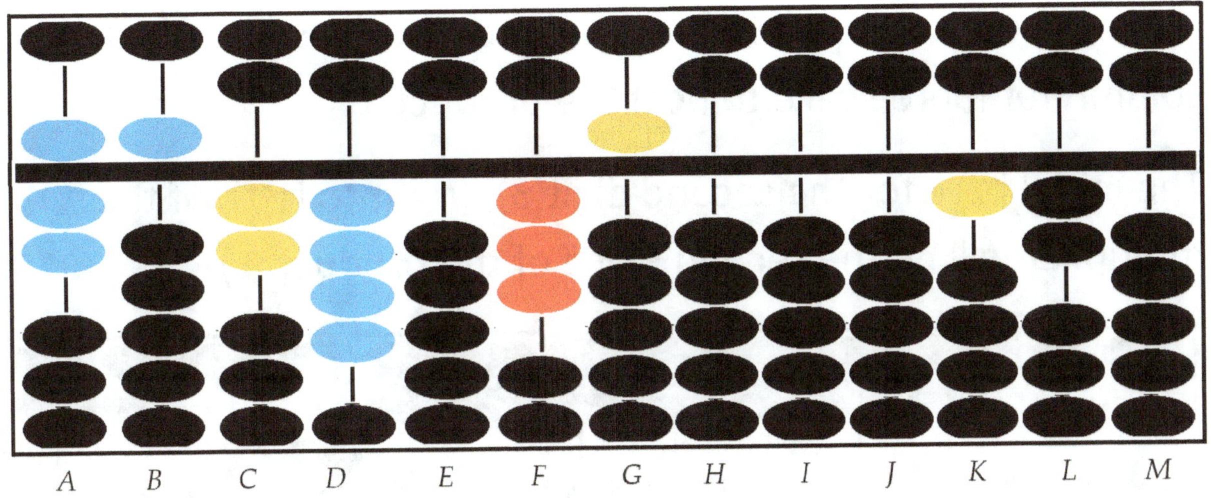

The base for C is L but it too is a zero of the 10.

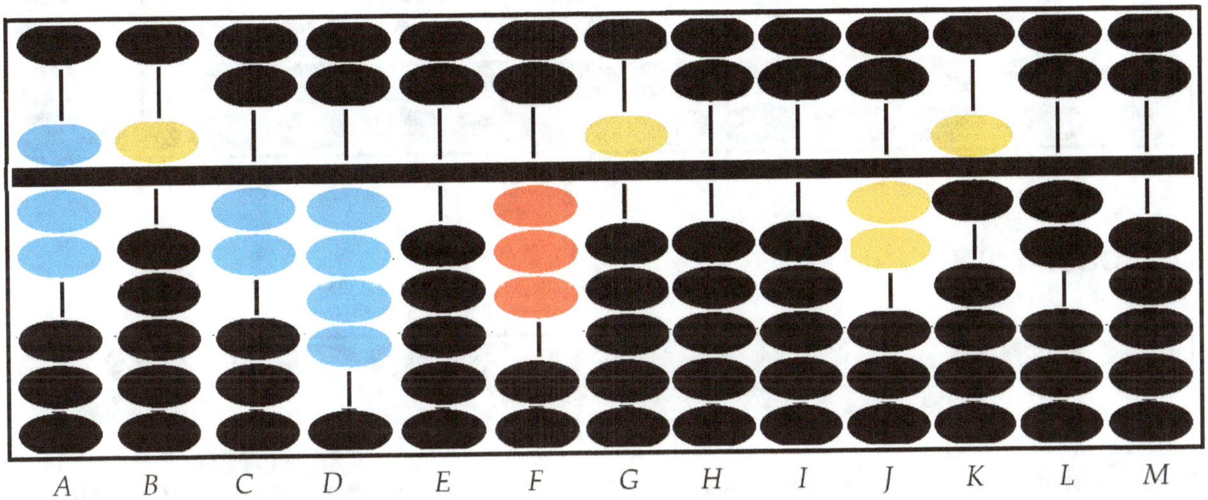

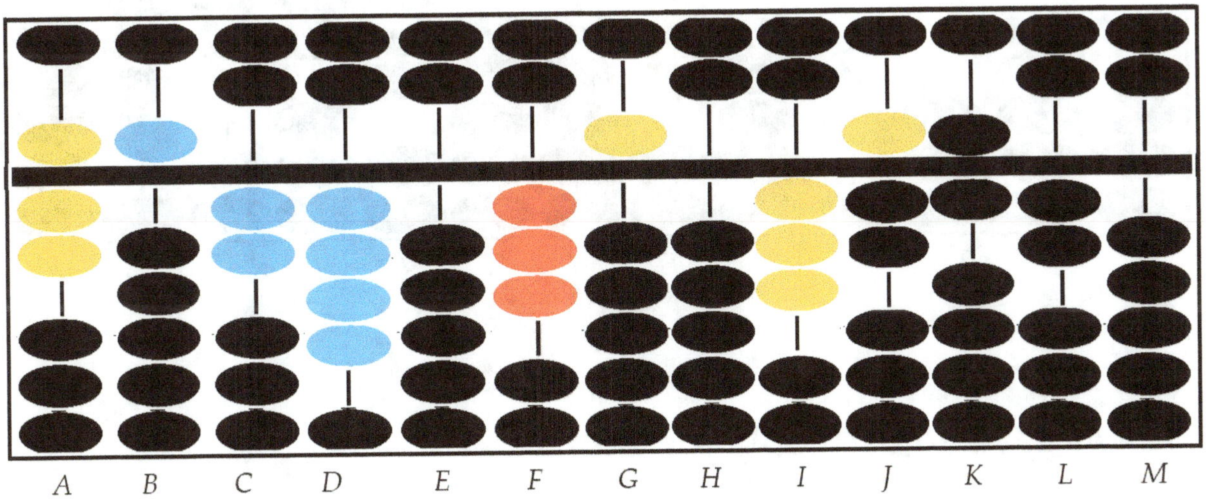

Having used the multiplier 5 all we need; we may reclaim the column for more space to post the product.

The initial base for the second digit(3), (right to left), of the multiplier will be the second place of the product (L).

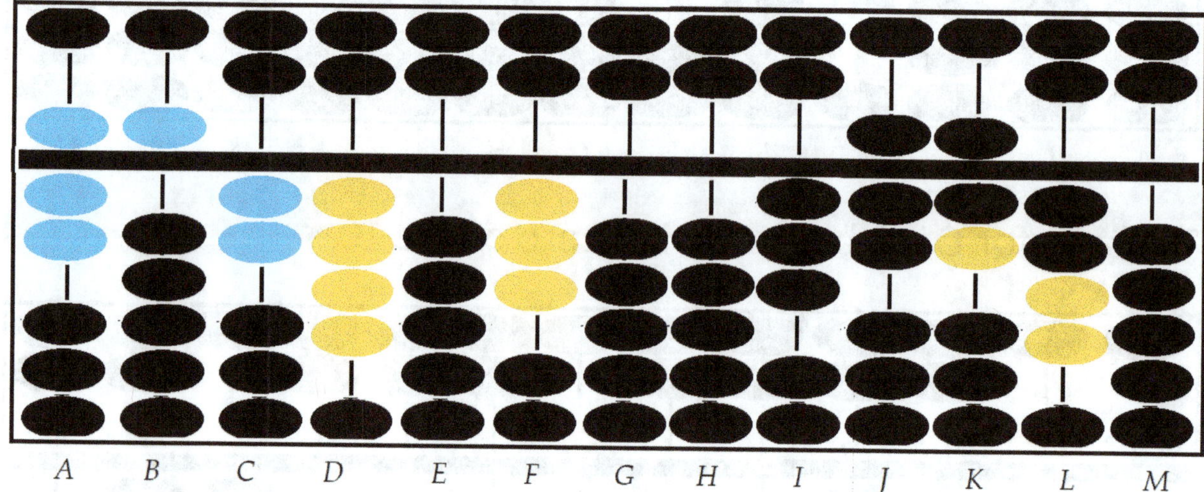

The base for C will be K

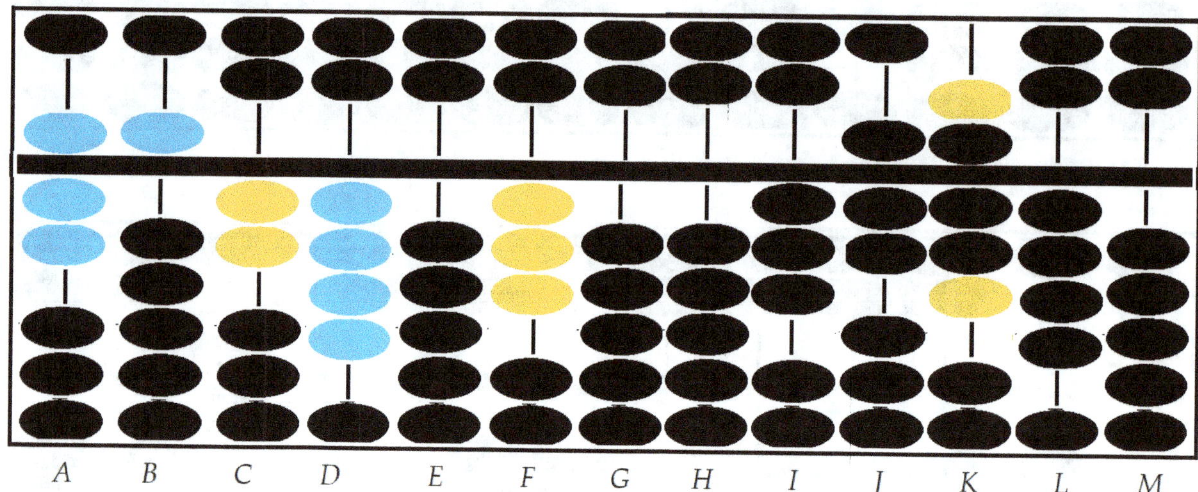

We will save adjustments for later.

For B the base is J

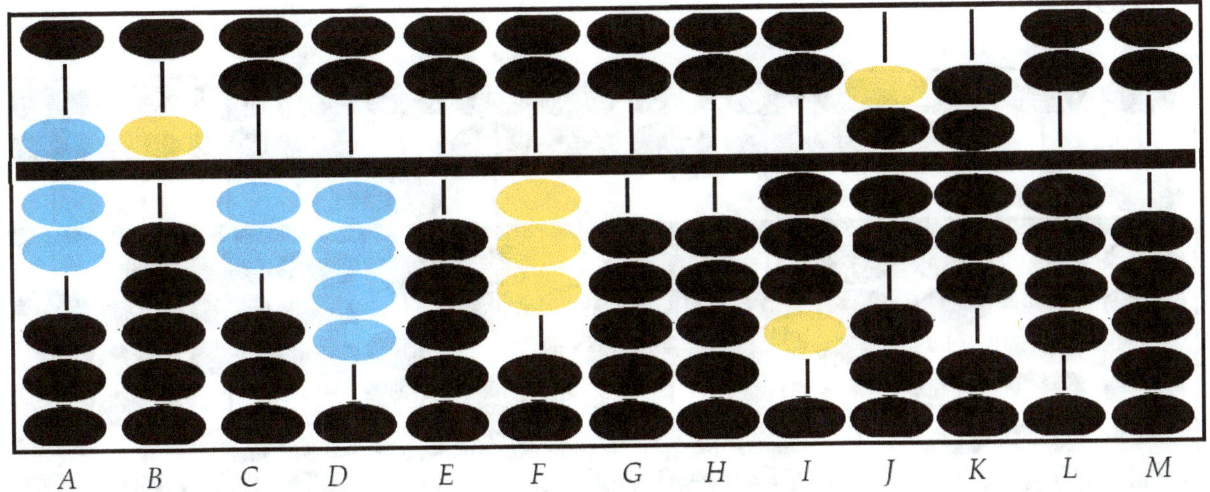

I is base for A

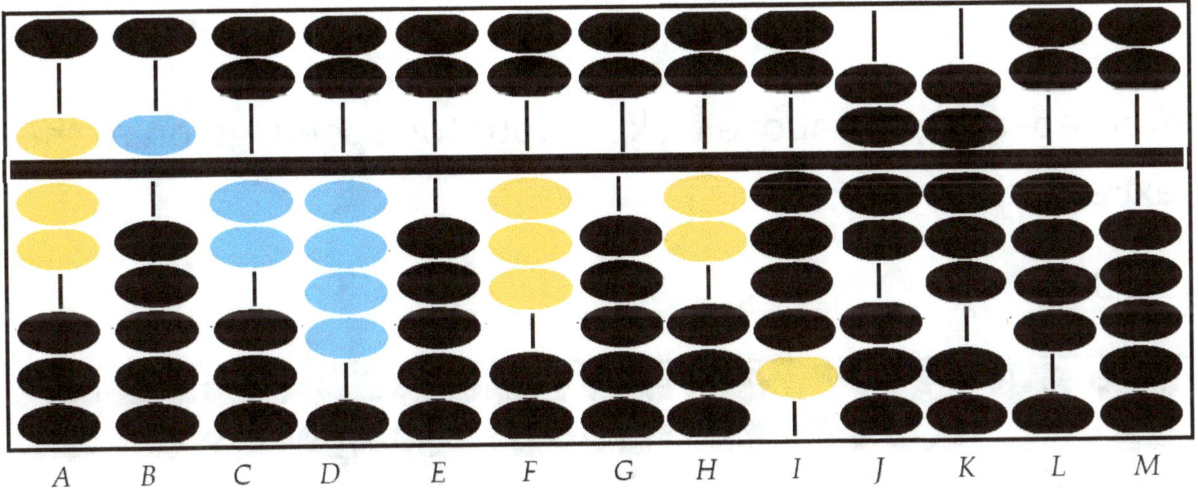

After replacing 5 ones with 1 five and 2 tens for 4 fives, the product is

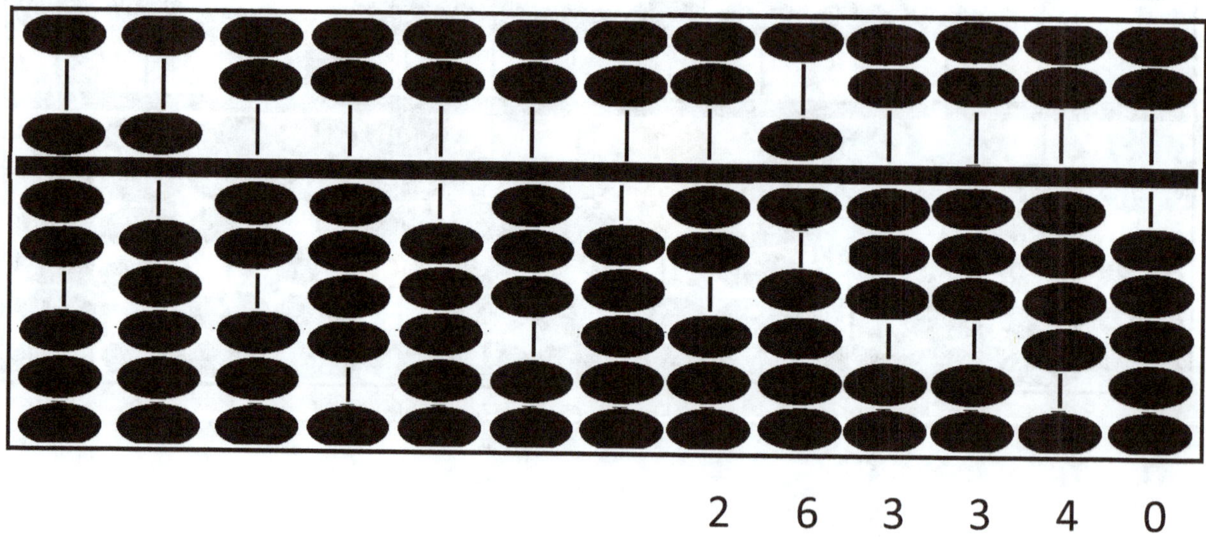

2   6   3   3   4   0

After repeating the above task, at your top speed, go on to the next exercise.

45 x 32

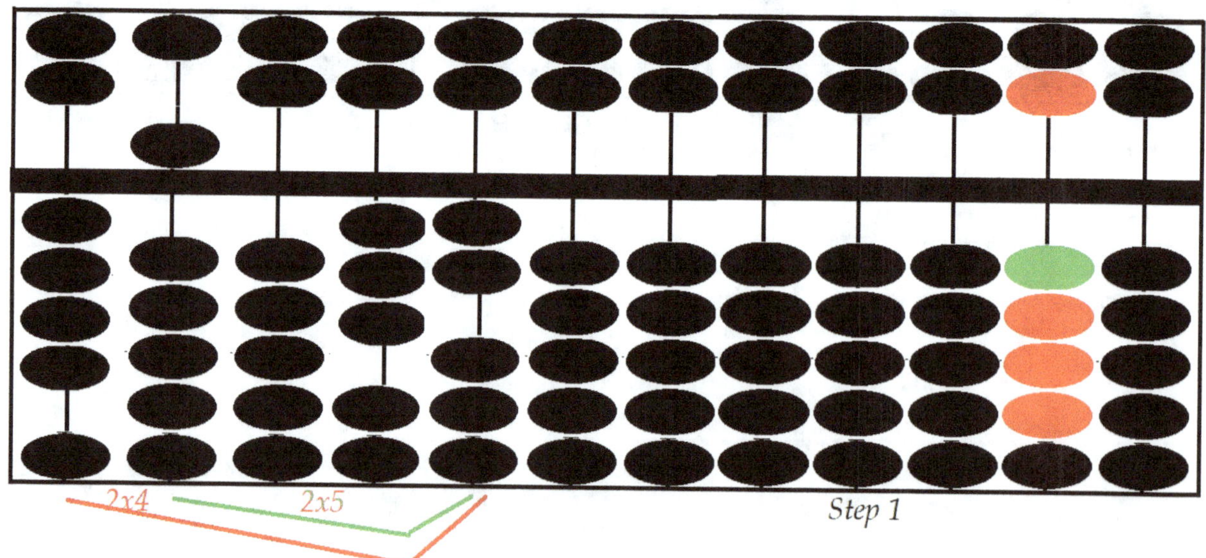

Step 1

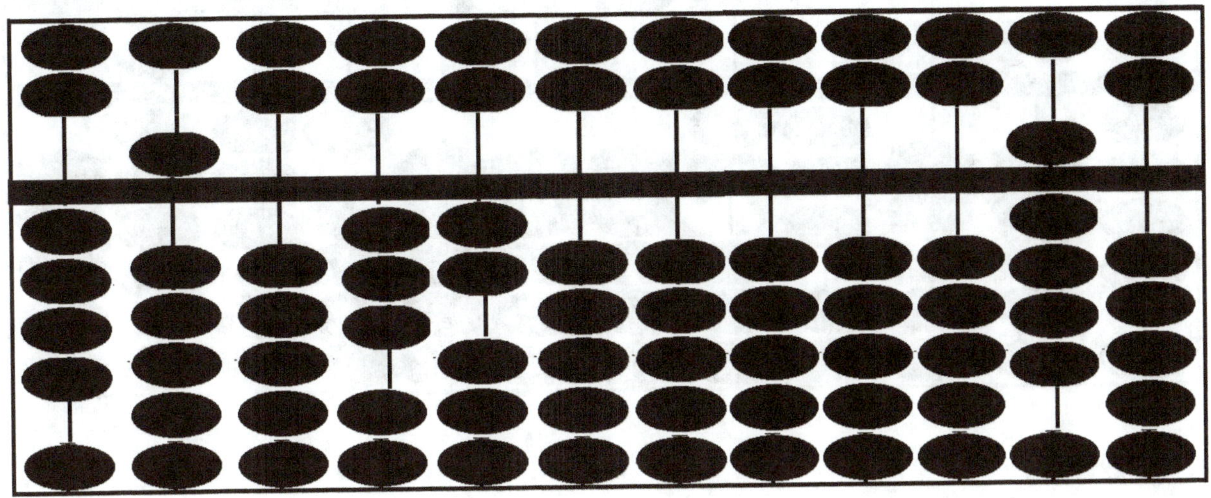

Step 2

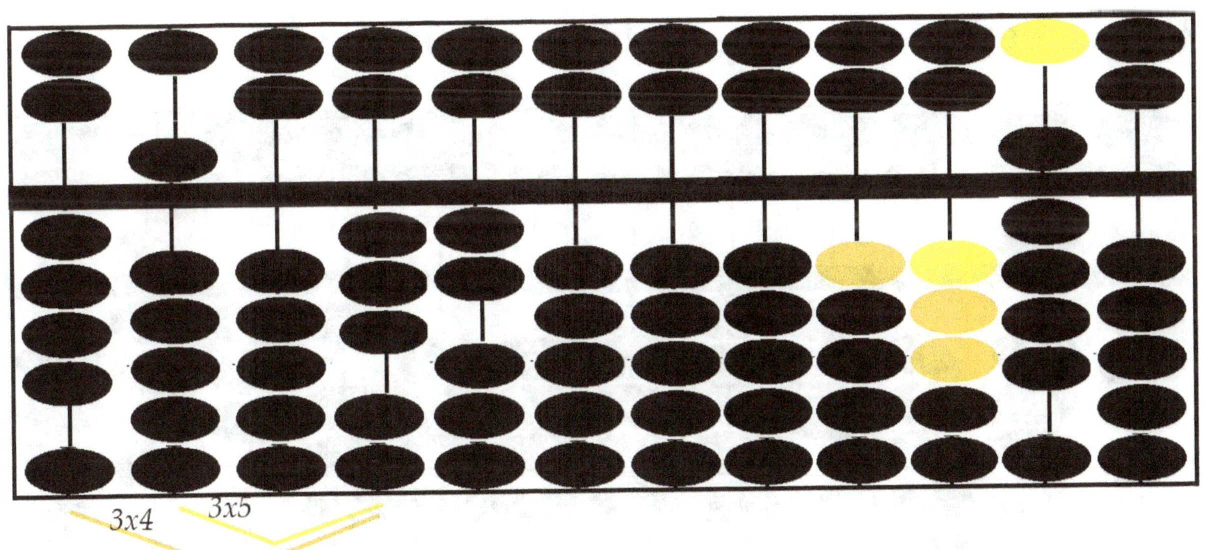

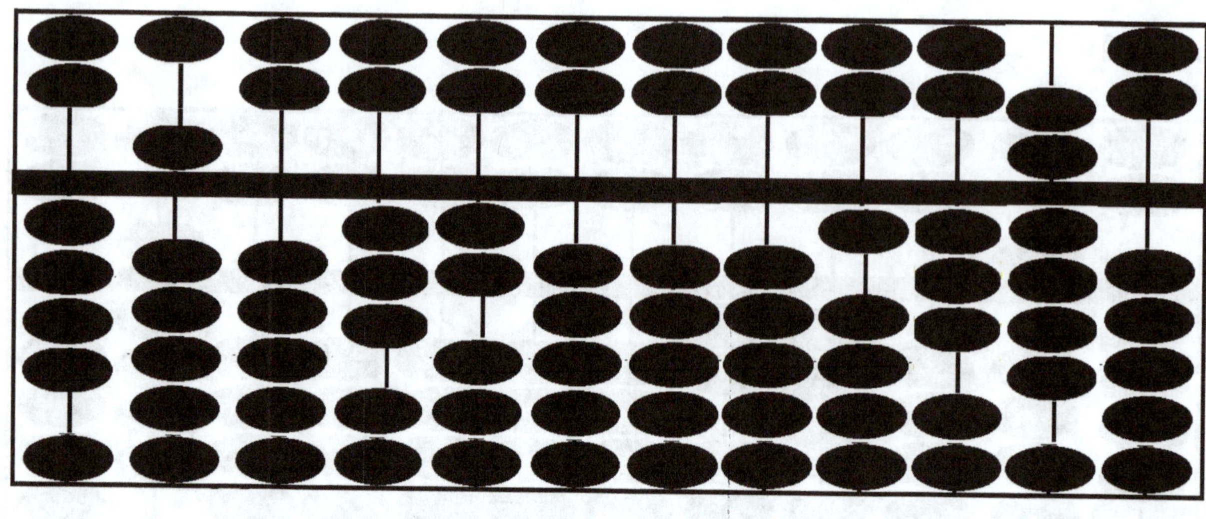

Replacement of two 50 beads by one 100 bead

Step3

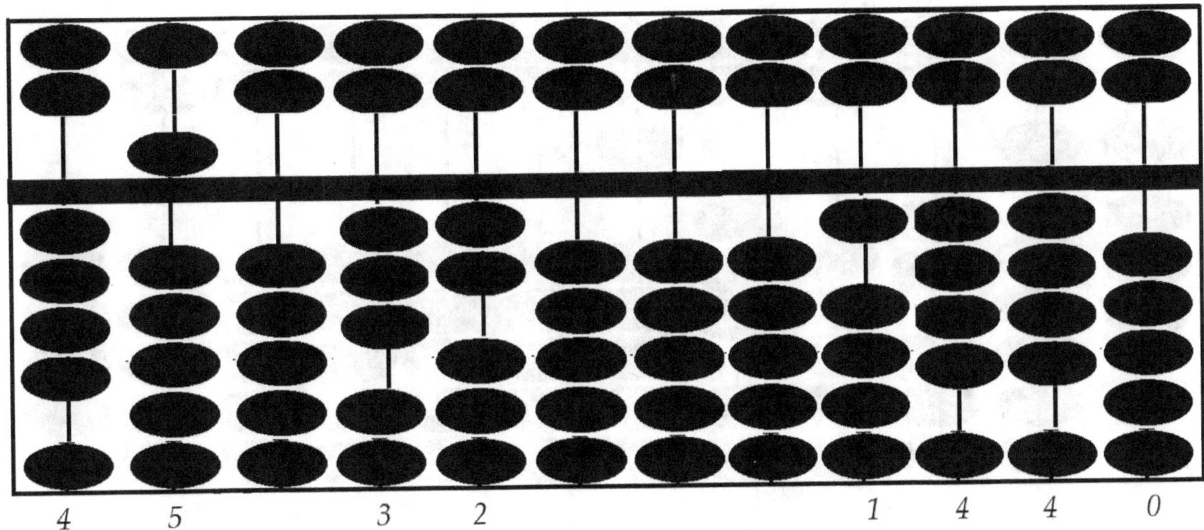

45 x 32 = 1,440

This one is yours.

6,394 x 25   Mark the beads to show your answer

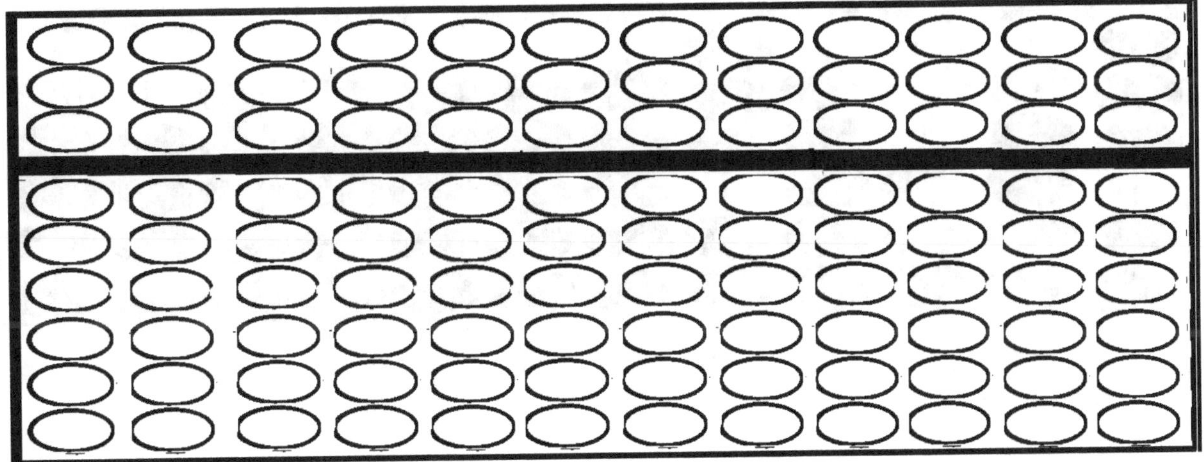

852 x 35

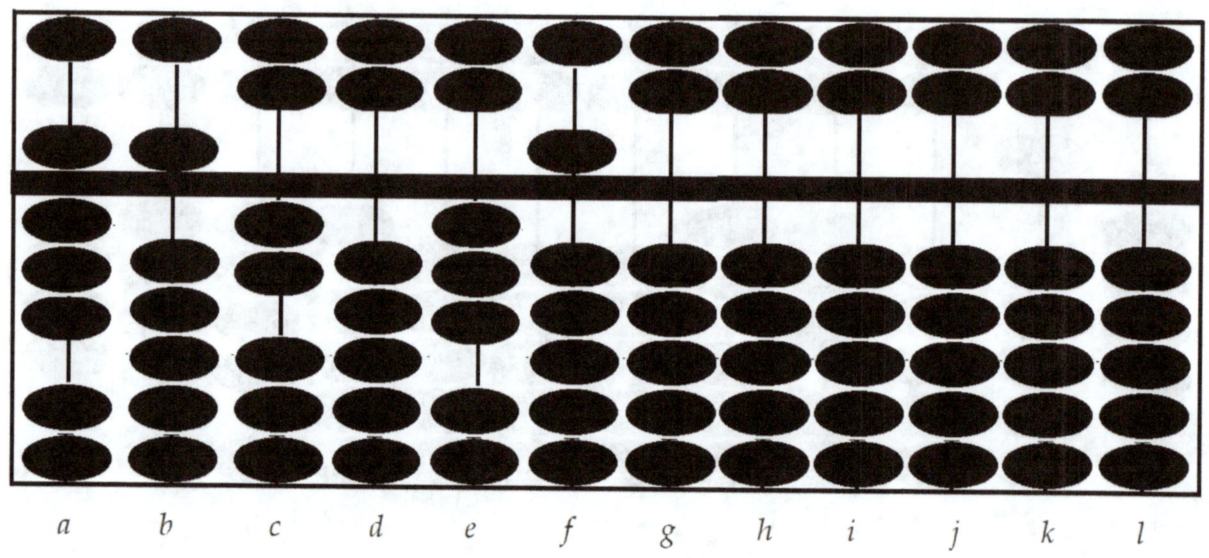

Step 1, f x c (base at l); f x b (base at k); f x a (base at j)

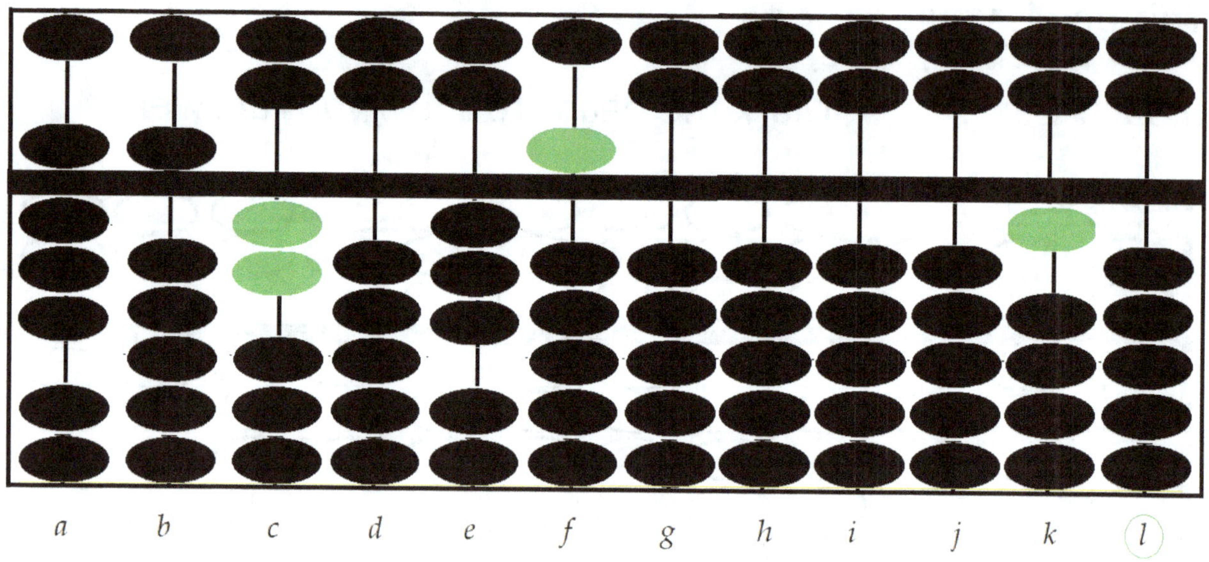

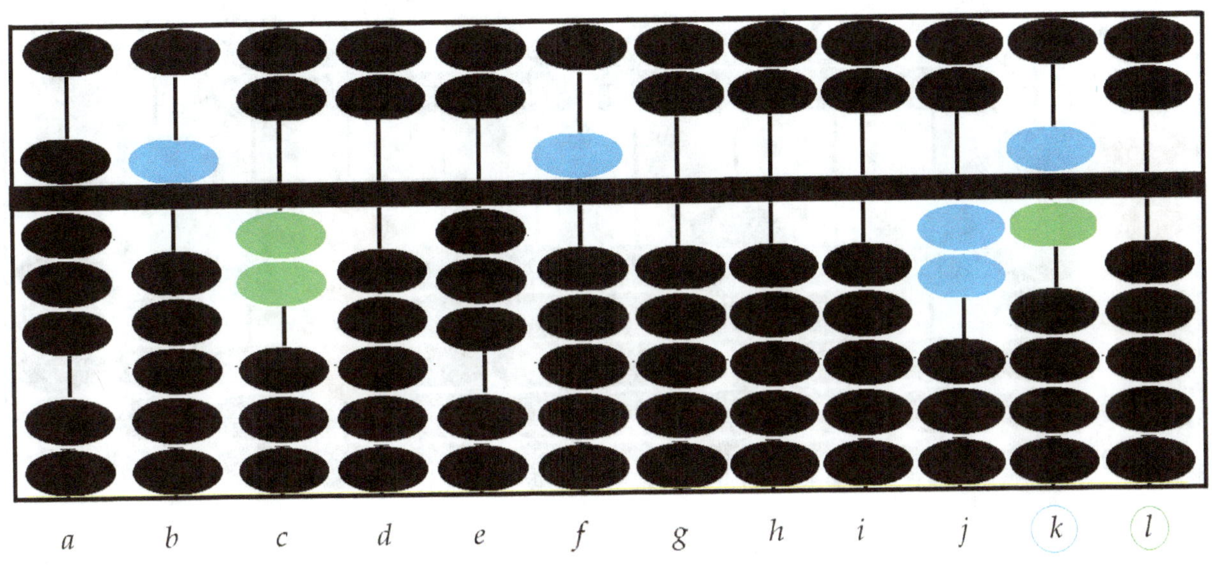

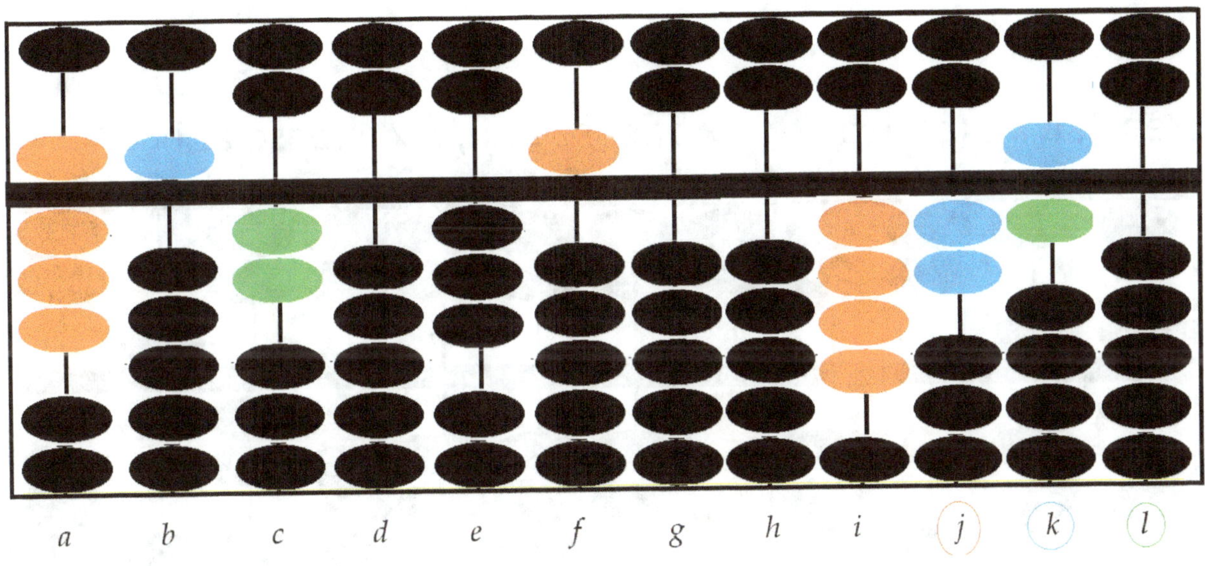

Again, having used the multiplier 5 all we need; we may reclaim the column for more space to post the product.

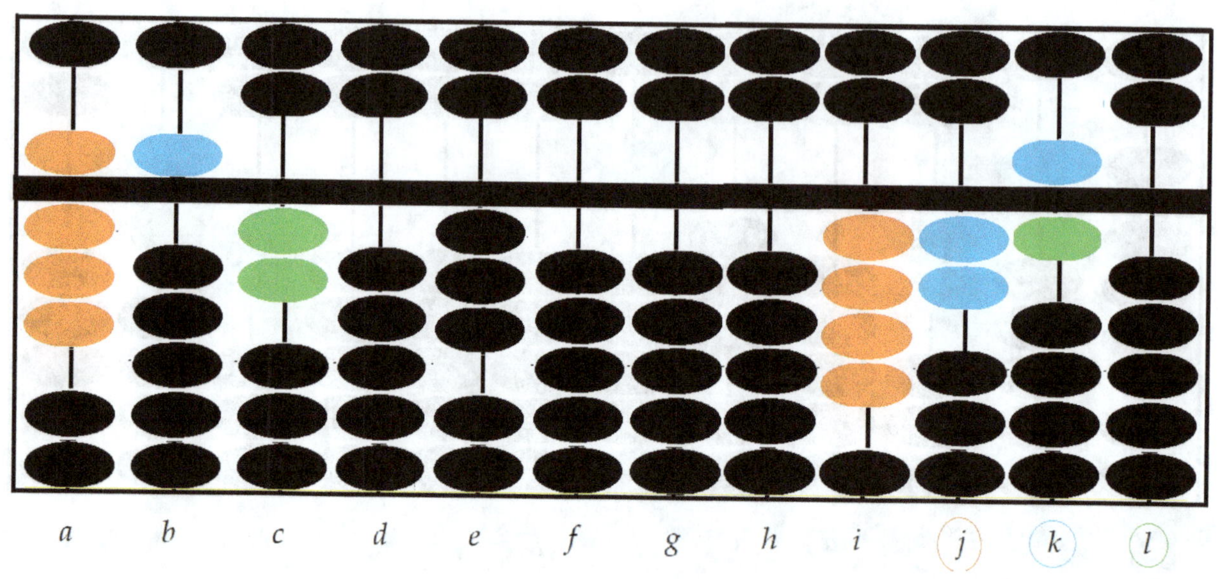

Step 2, e x c (base at k); e x b (base at j); e x a (base at i)

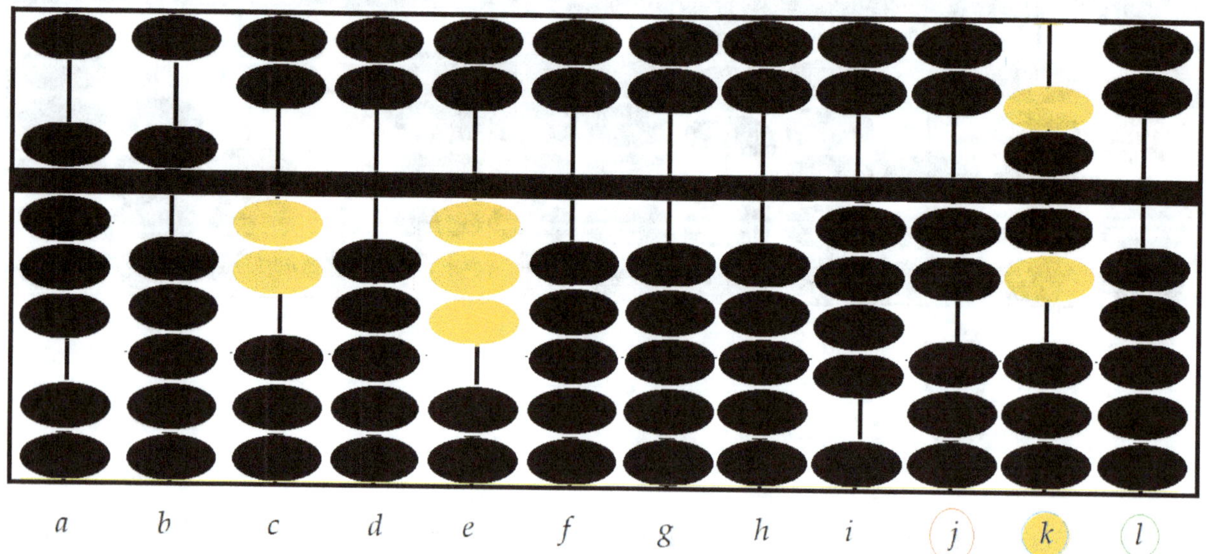

Make Reductions and replacements as you go.

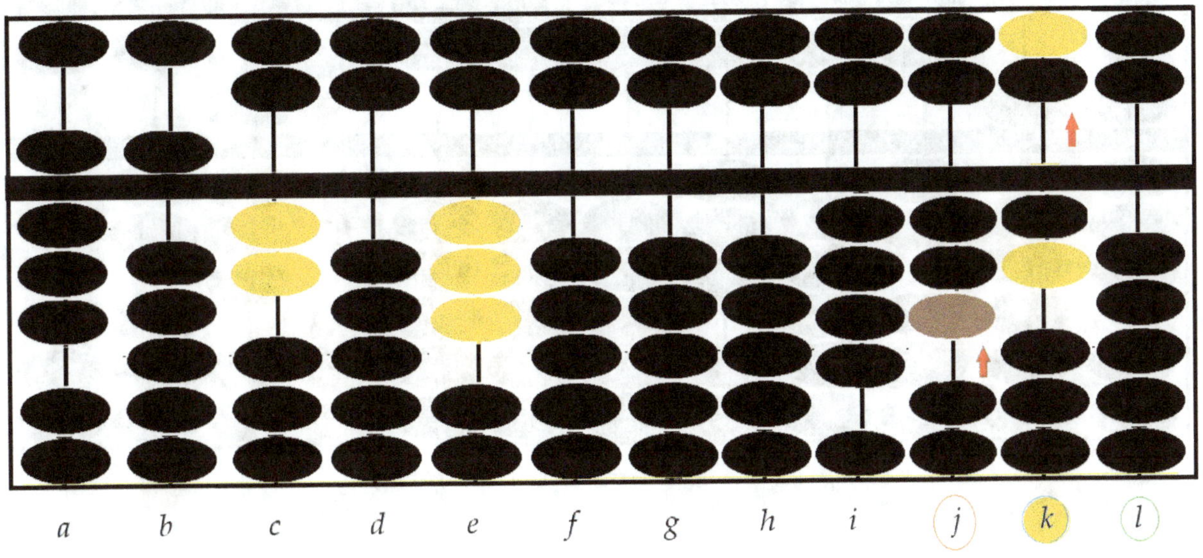

3 x 5 = 15 (base at j)

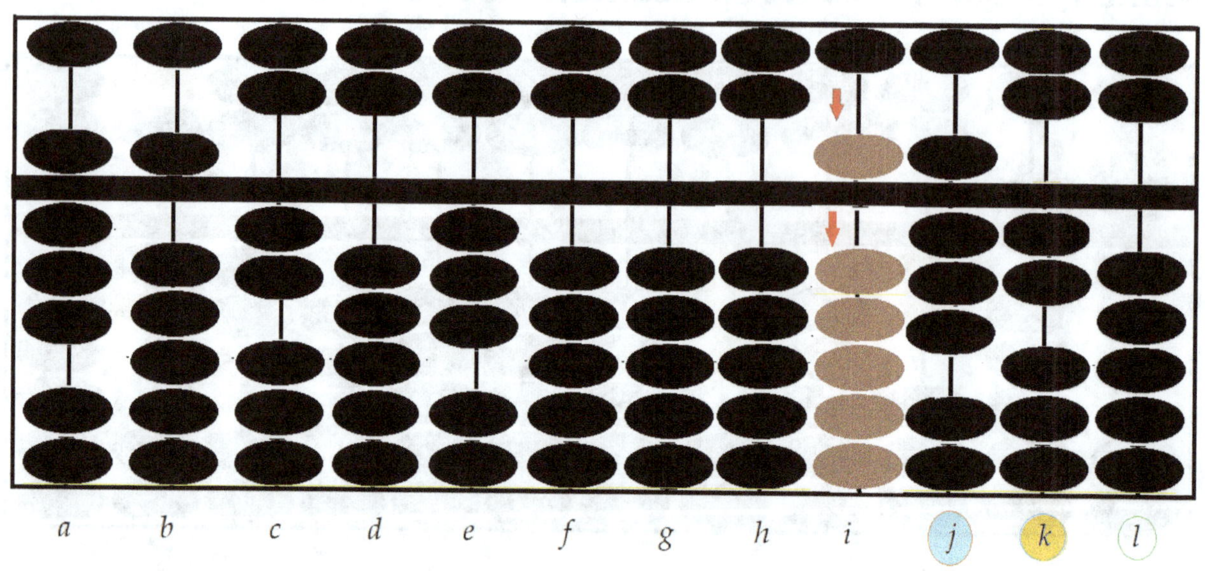

3 x 8 = 24 (base at i)

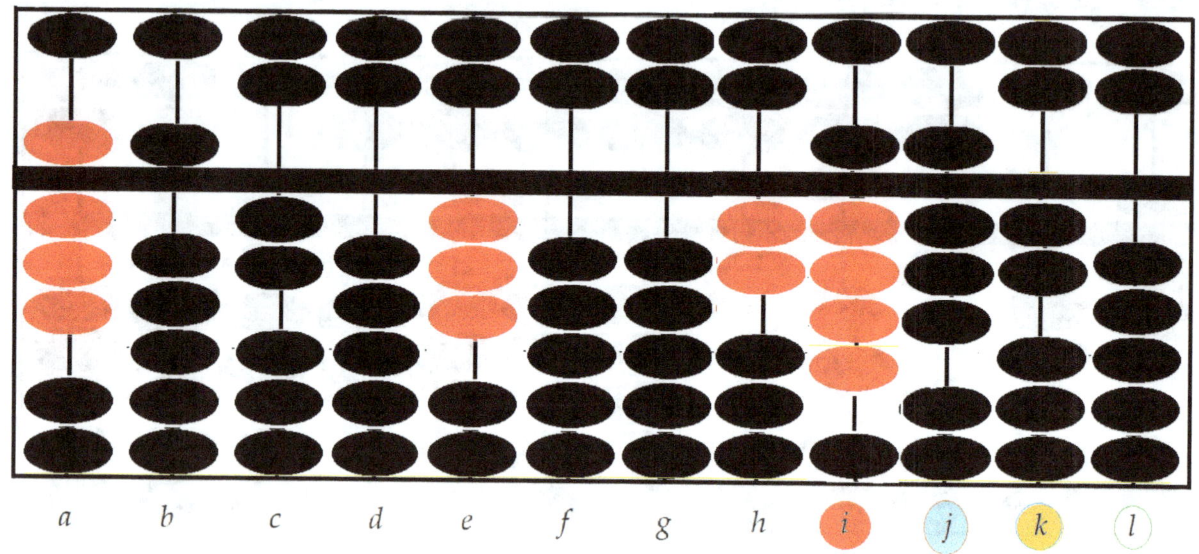

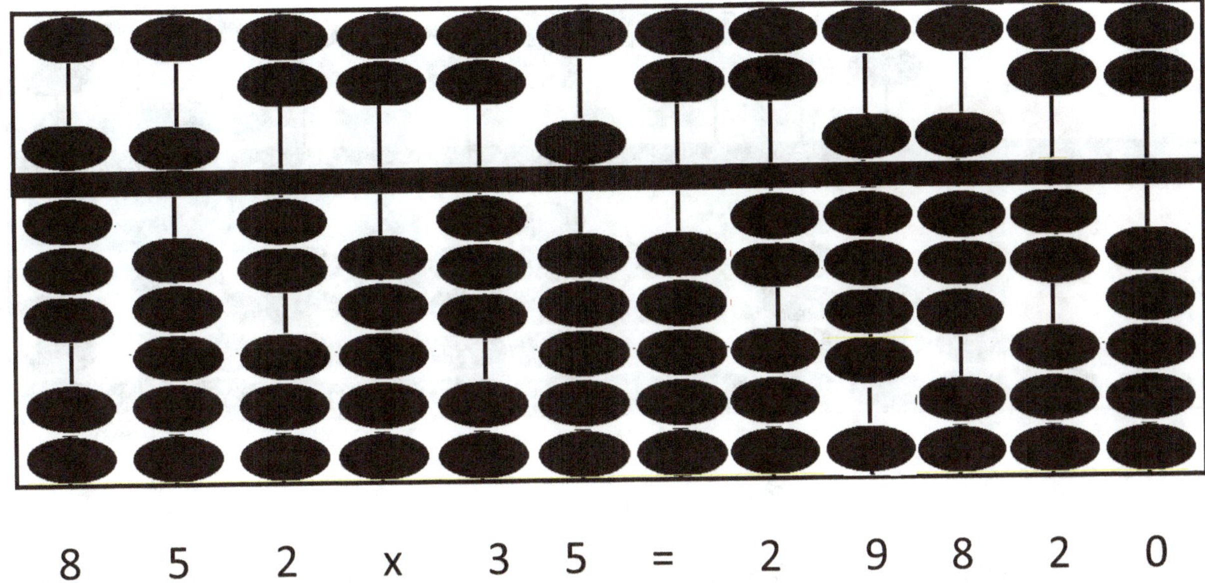

8   5   2   x   3   5   =   2   9   8   2   0

Can you do the above calculation in 15 seconds? Test yourself.

Try this one, with a stop watch. Set all beads to zero then go.

3,952 x 46

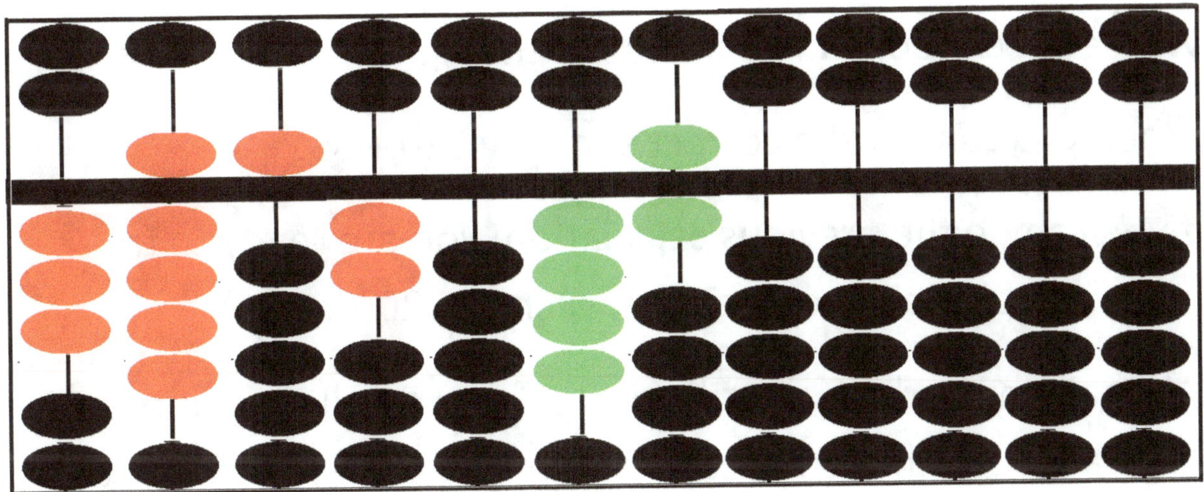

3, 9 5 2 x 4 6 = 1 8 1, 7 9 2

I added columns to make room for the product here, but you may reclaim multiplier spaces when they are no longer needed.

Try the same calculation and see if you can improve your speed. Your hand is being trained; so develop the habit of using the same finger or thumb for pushing up and pushing down beads.

With eyes closed, add 52 and 39 in the rightmost columns.

When you can get the correct sum; try 520 + 39.

If you can do the previous calculation; you are ready to try more complex blind operations, such as 520 + 390

We train in hand eye coordination. If you do all of your required calculations with the abacus you may increase you skill to the level of "touch typing" or "ten key by touch".

Practice:

289 x 20 =   54 x 18 =   108 x 42 =

128 x 15 =   490 x 26 =   3,428 x 37 =

245 x 11 =   1,830 x 91 =   23,100 x 12 =

3 Digits multiplier

184 x 216

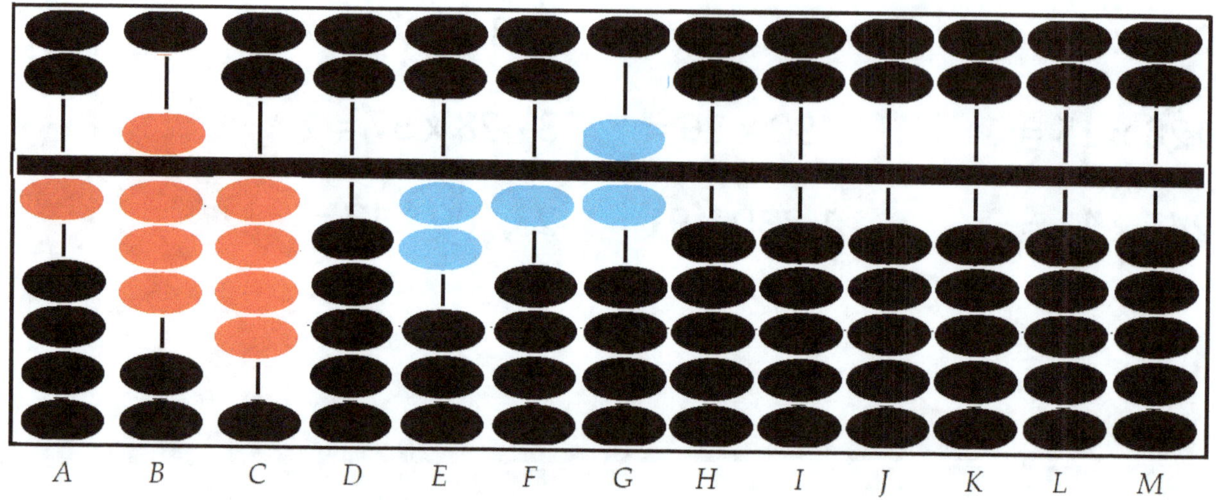

6 X 4 = 24 (base at M)

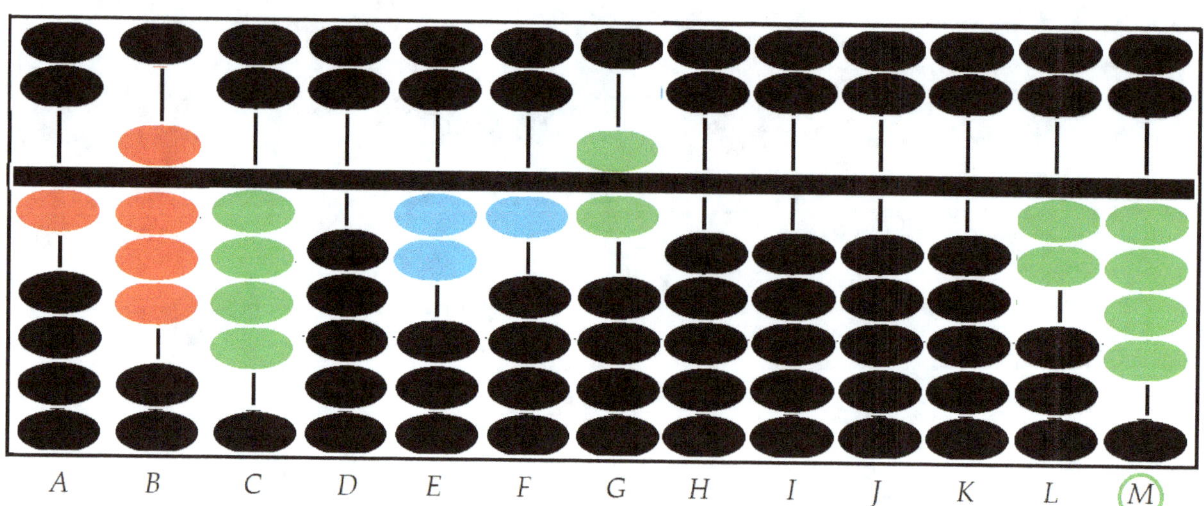

6 x 8 = 48 (base at L)

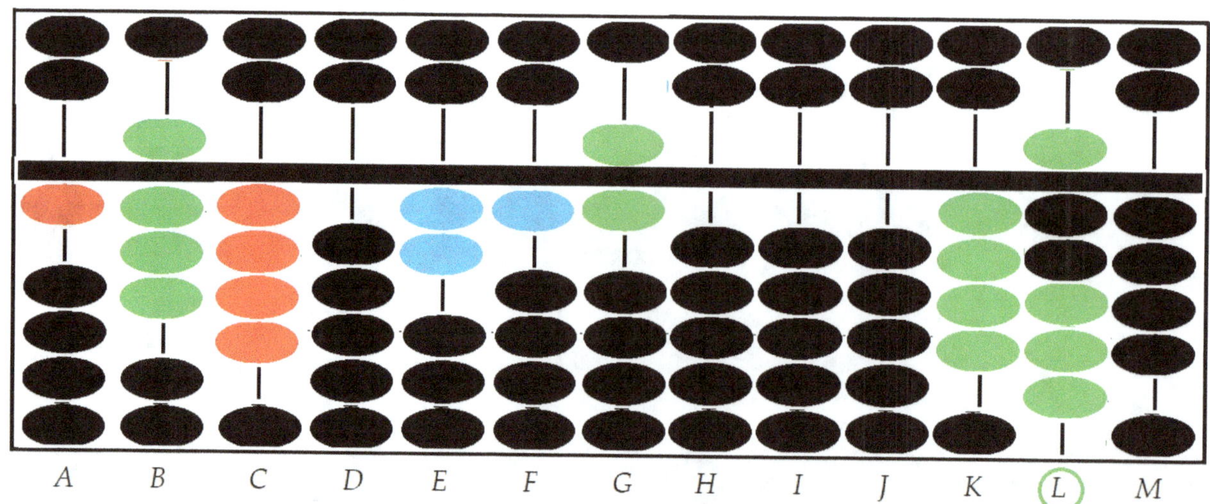

Adjustments as you go

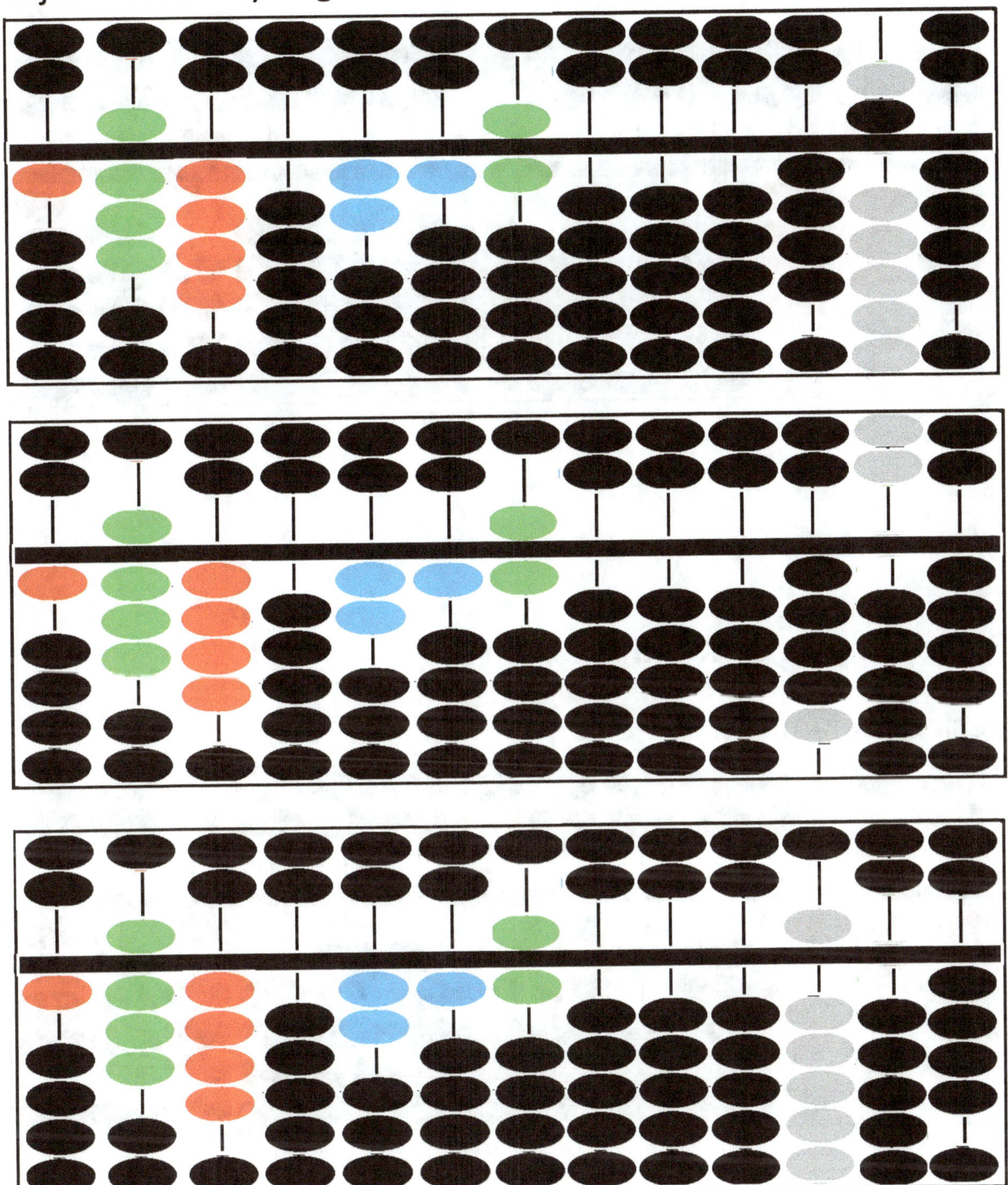

6 x 1 = 6 (base at K)

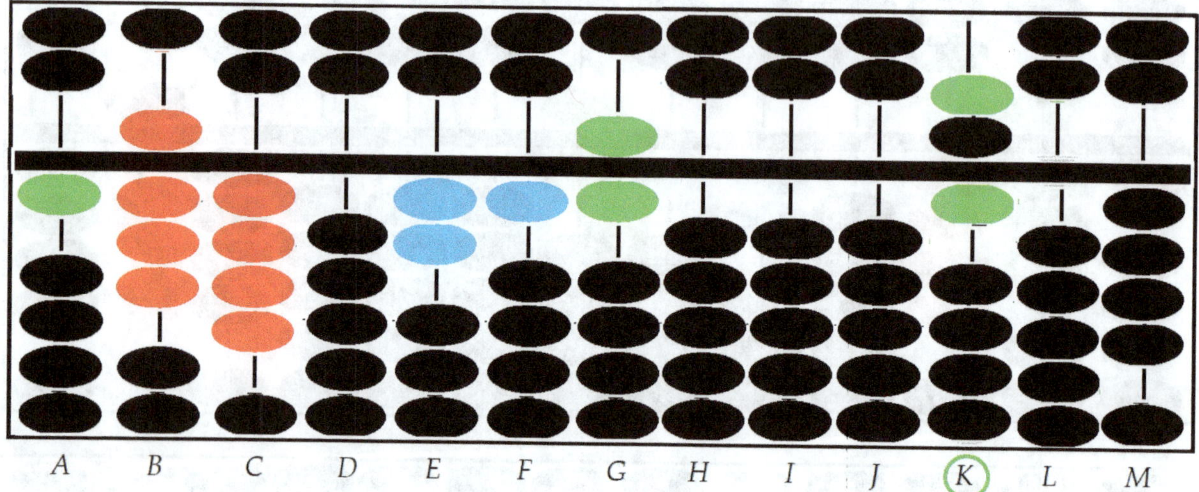

Replace 2 fives on K with a ten on J.

Reclaim column on G.

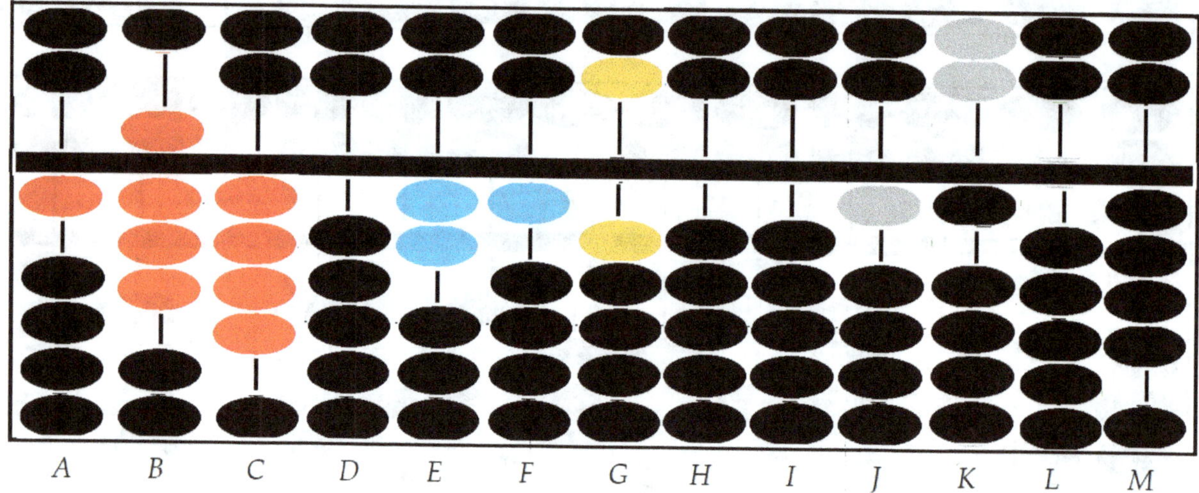

1 x 184 = 184 (base at L)

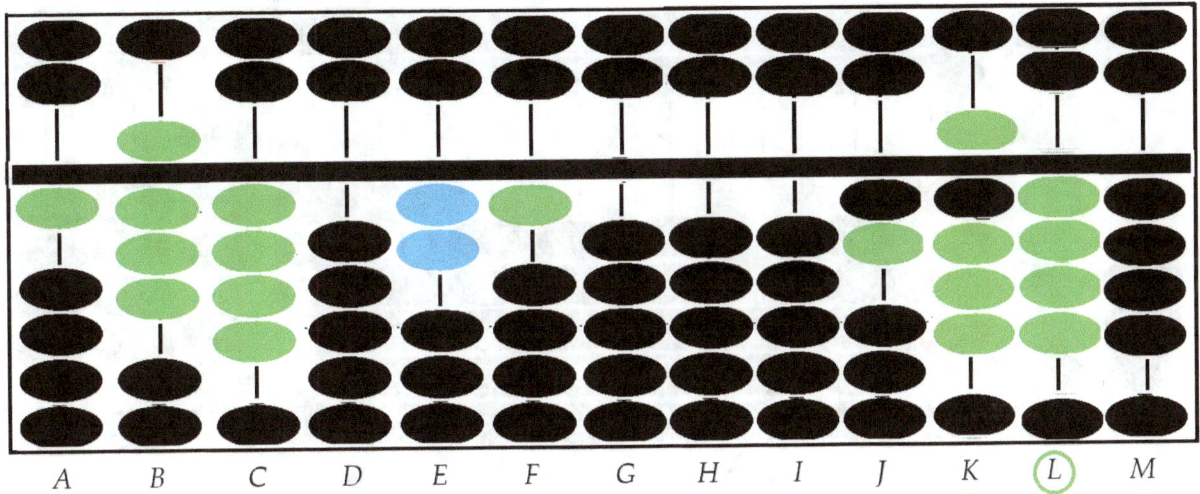

2 x 4 = 8 (base at K) Beads not available for 8 on K so you add

10 on J and subtract 2 on K. (+10 − 2 = + 8)

You reclaimed column F, creating more space for the product.

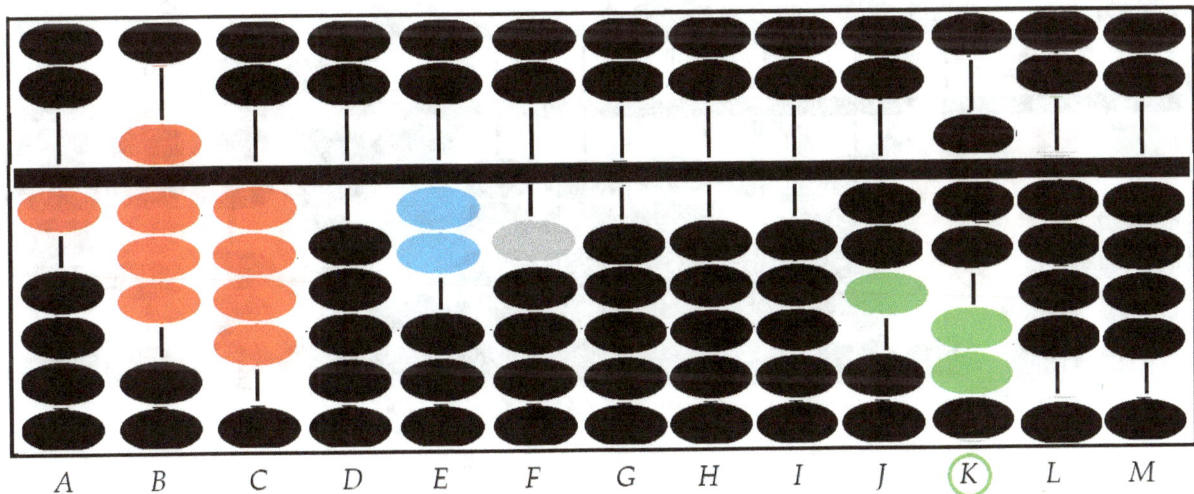

2 x 8 = 16 (base at J)

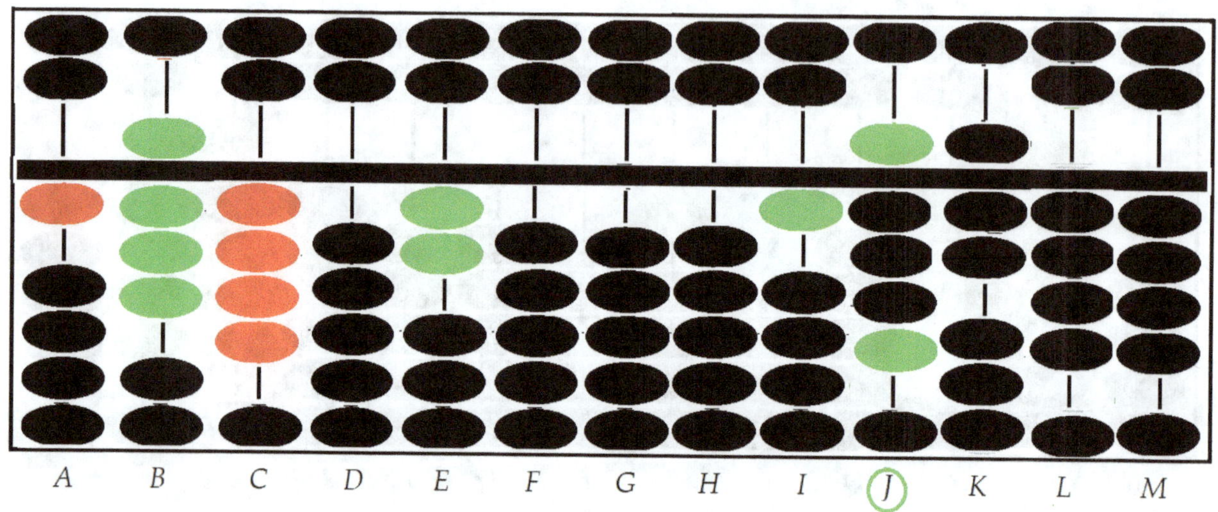

2 x 1 = 2 (base at I)

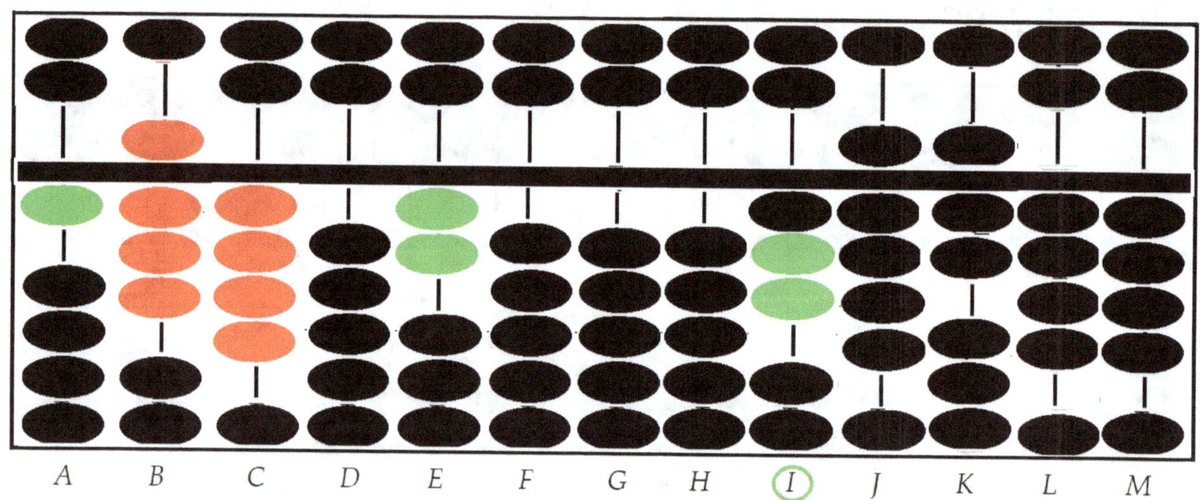

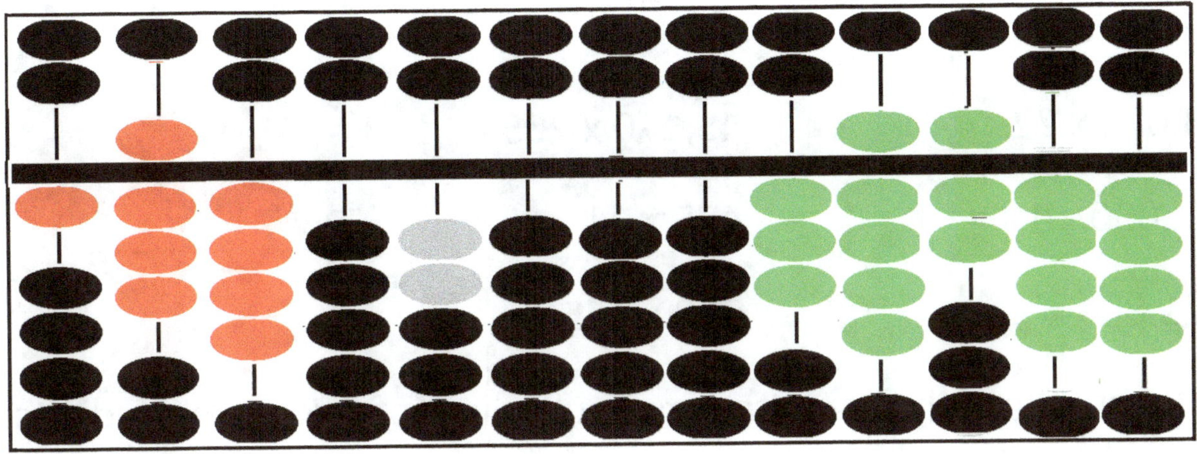

184 x 216 = 39,744

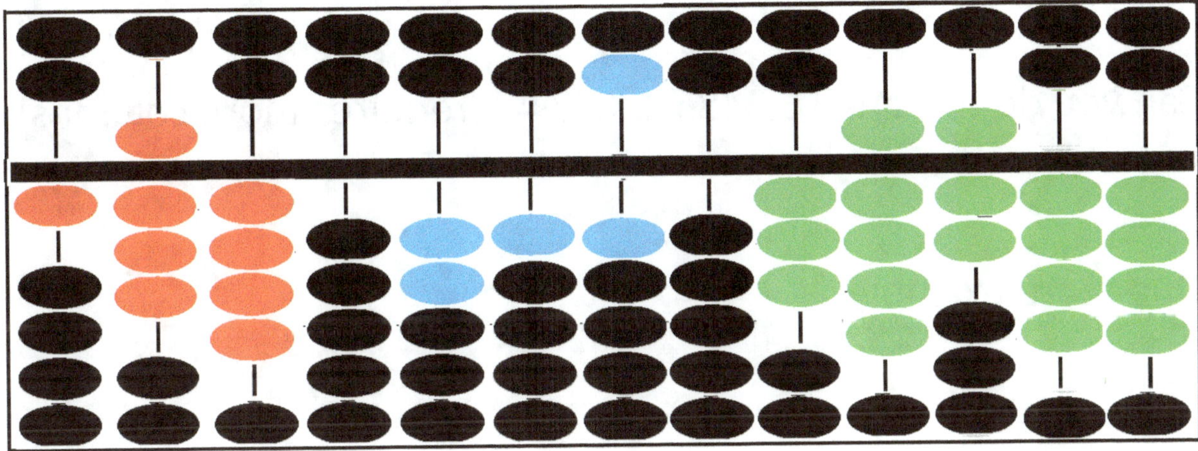

We didn't need the extra spaces created by reclaiming columns when we were through with the multiplier digits on them, but now we know how to; if we need them next time.

Repeat the previous calculation 3 times from scratch and see if practice increases your speed.

Practice:

3,074 x 223 =   45,170 x 205 =

9, 090 x 18 =   475 x 21 =   62 x 7 =

21,804 x 12 =   718 x 465 =

The rules are the same for any multipliers of two or more digits.

Can you do this one? 5,348 x 1,607 =   (requires more columns)

One more example:

4,856 x 3.14

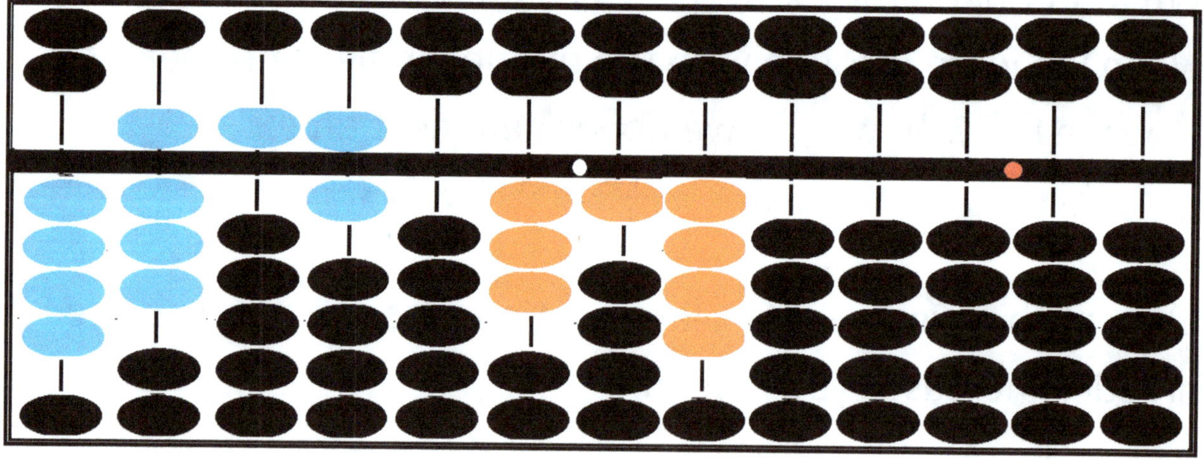

I am allowing for 2 decimal places in the product.

4 x 6

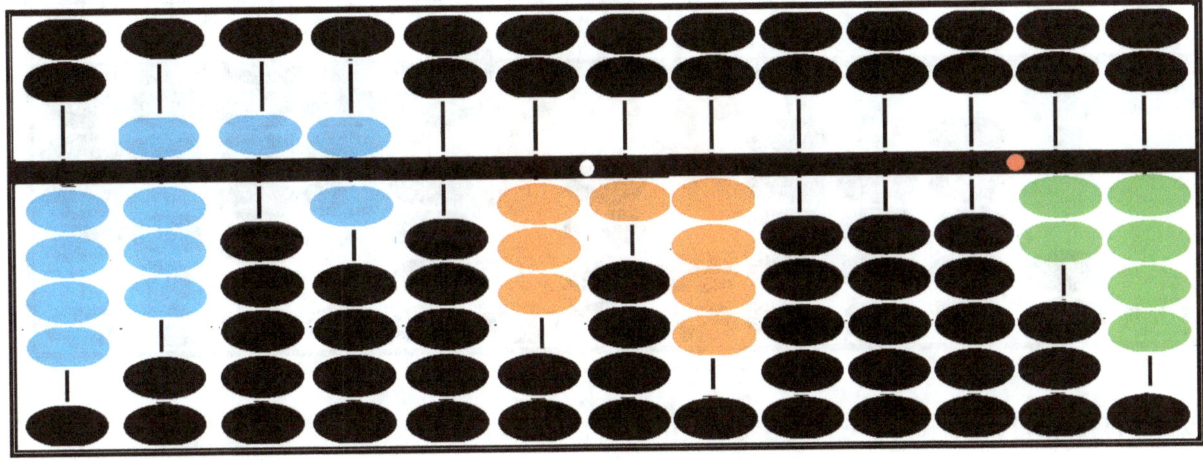

4 x 5

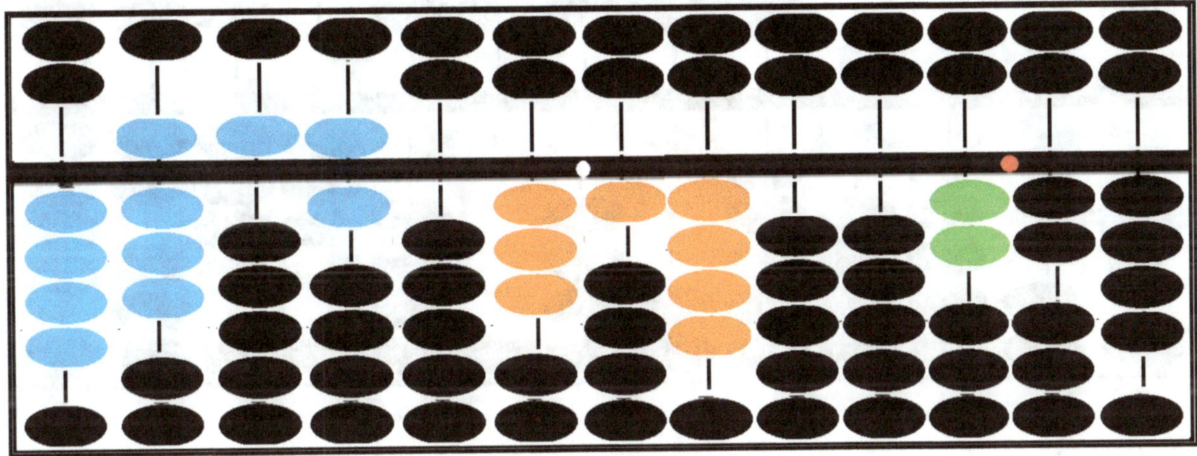

4 x 8

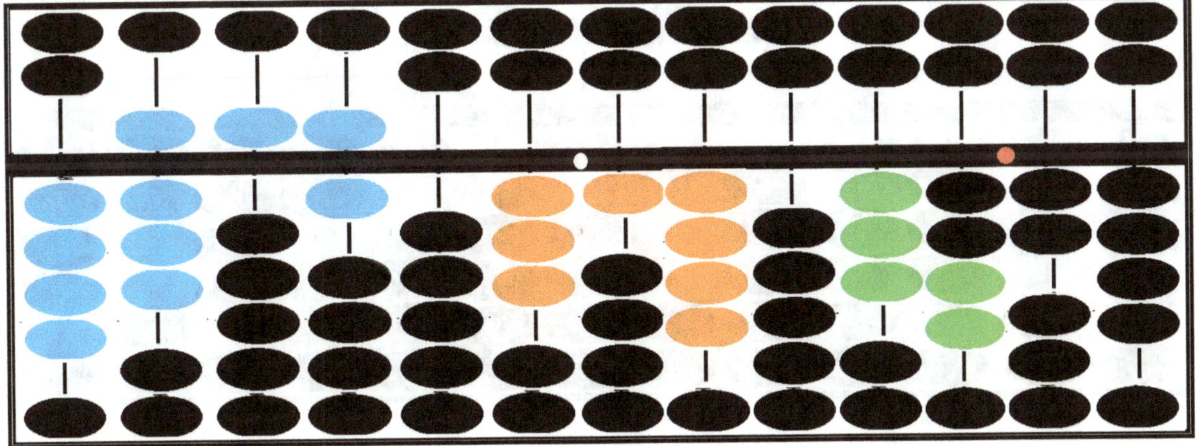

4 x 4

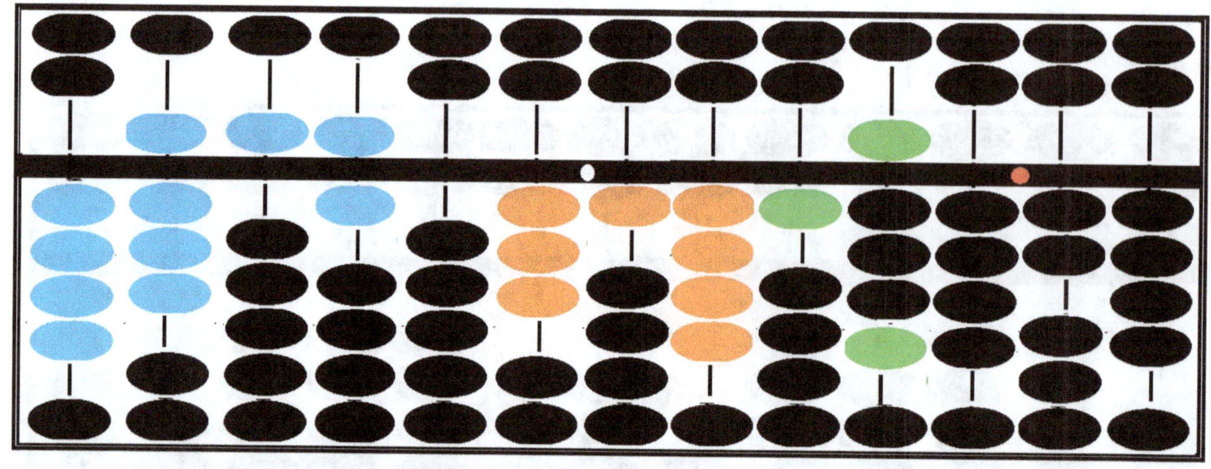

We may need the extra column!

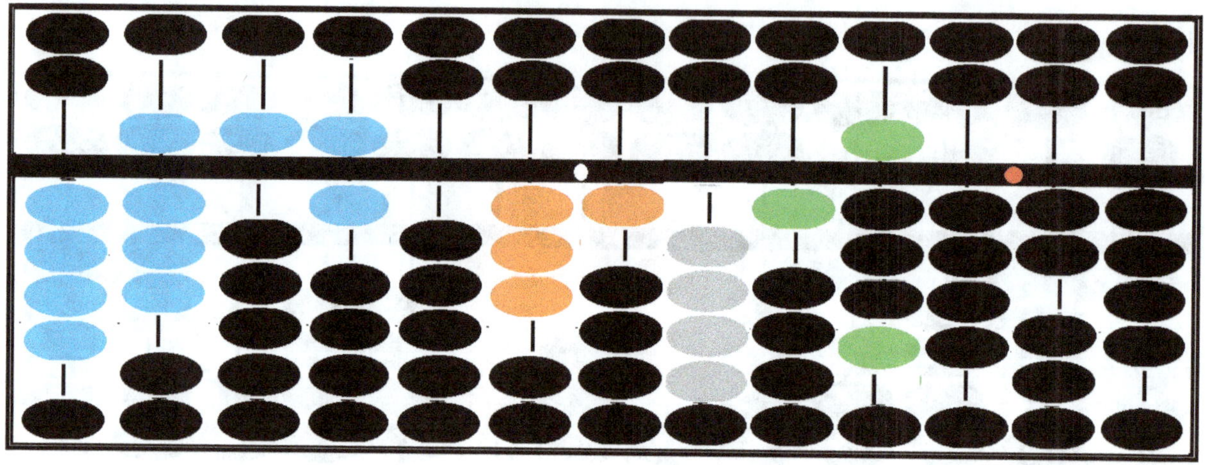

1 x 4856

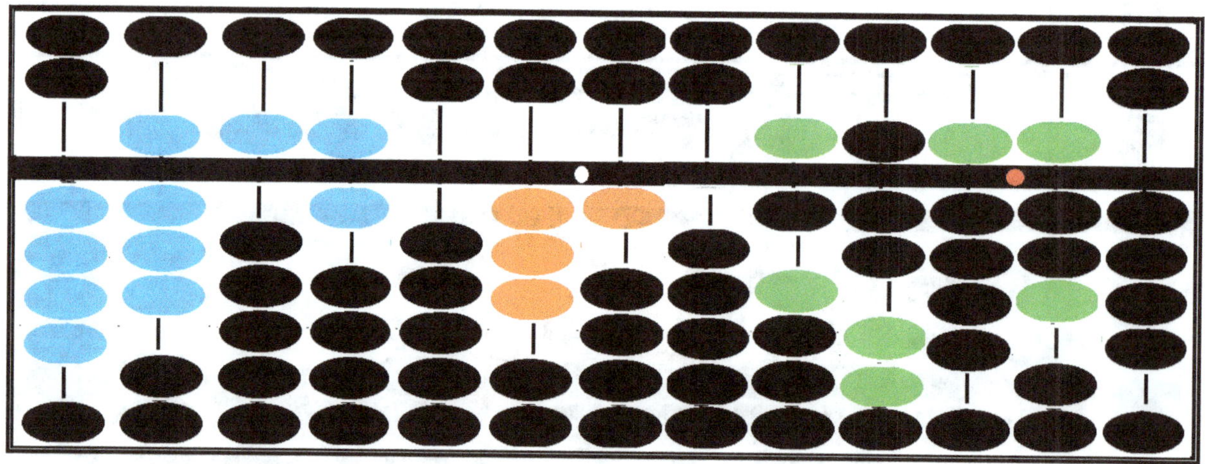

3 x 6

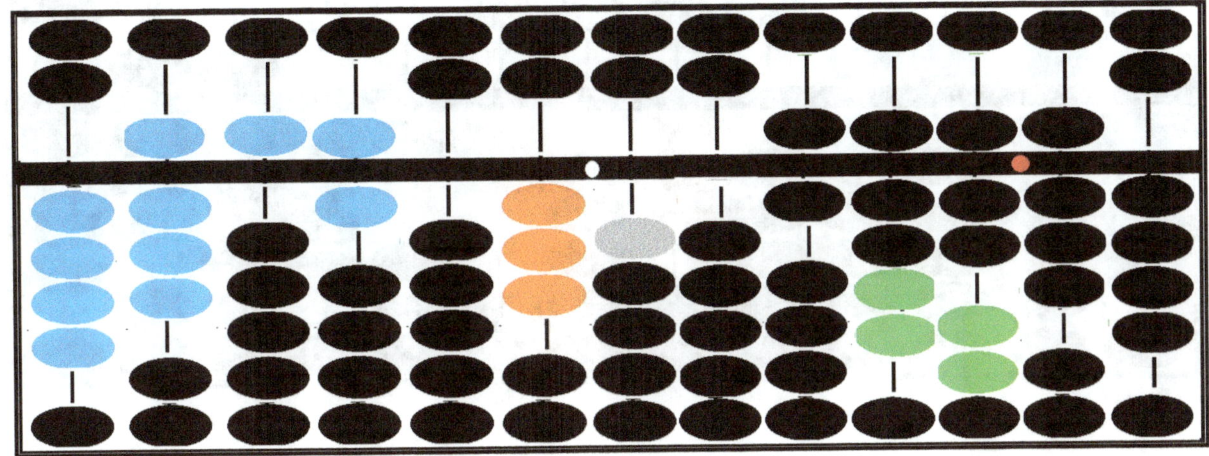

3 x 5

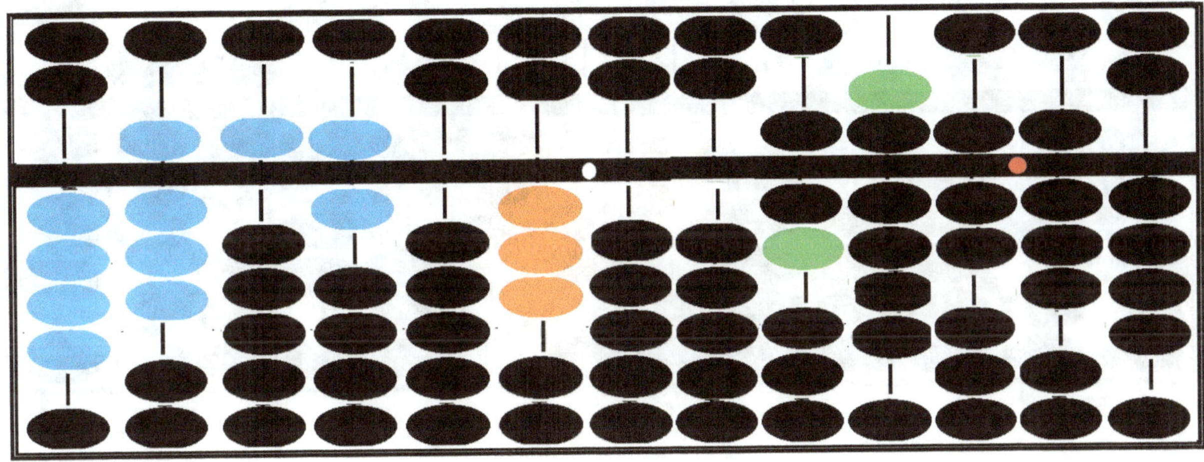

3 x 8

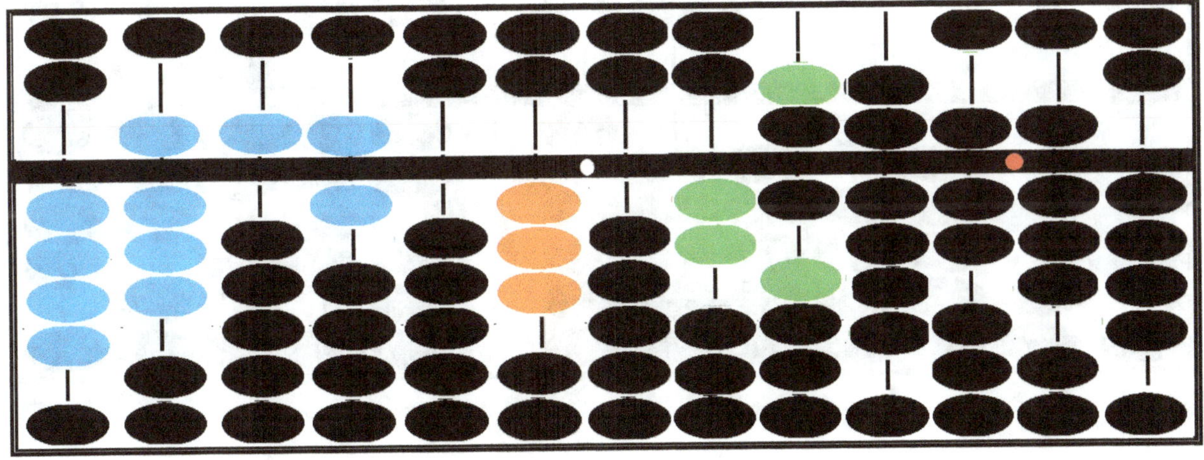

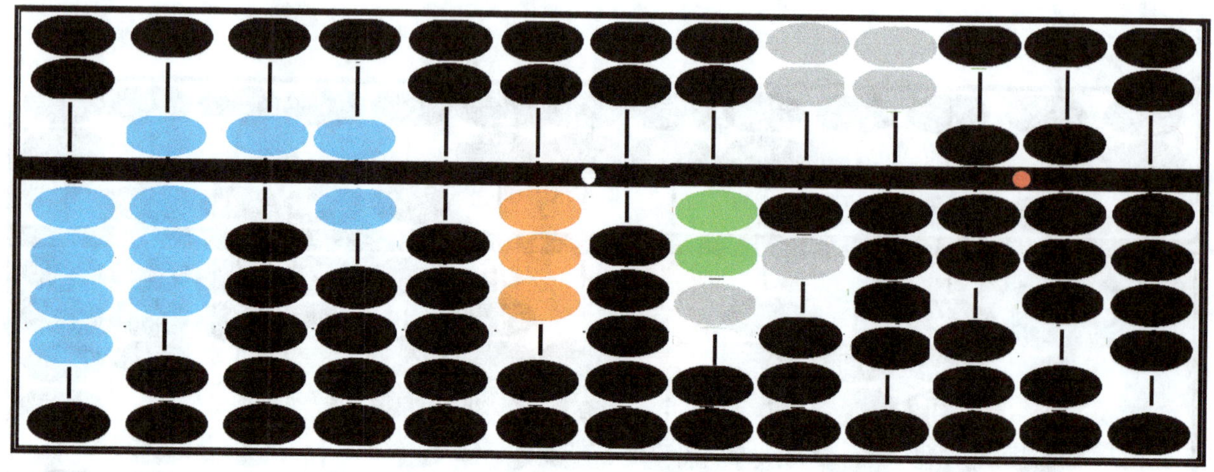

3 x 4

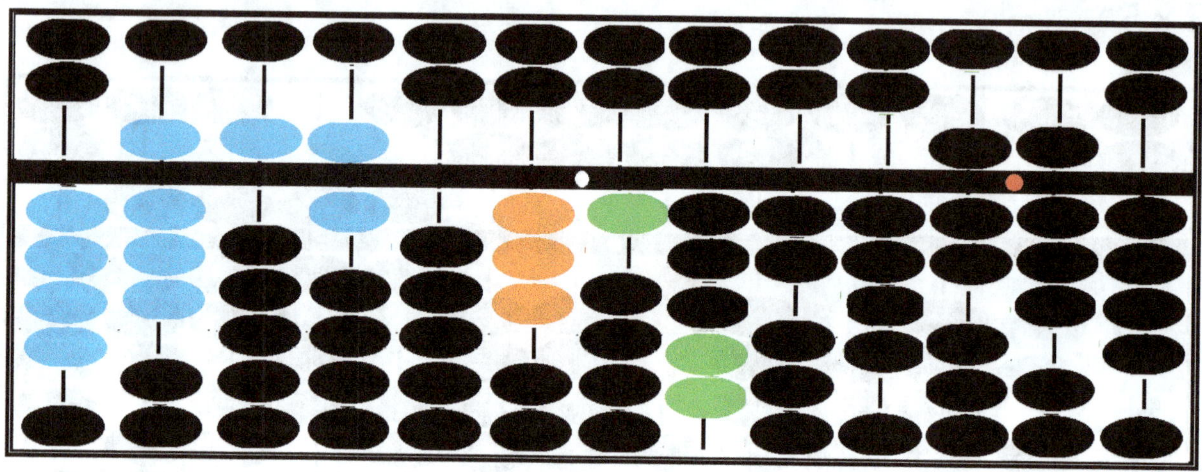

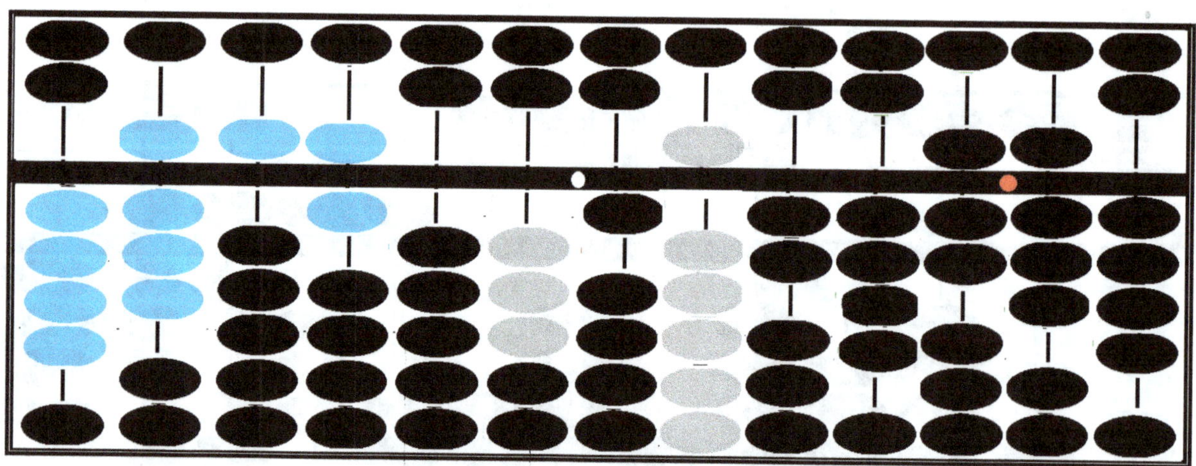

4,856 x 3.14 = 15,247.84

DIVISION

The Quotient grows from left to right.

Set the dividend on the right; skip one or more columns to the left and set the divisor. Estimate the number of decimal places according to the degree of accuracy required for your purpose.

Quotient   Divisor   Dividend

When we have a Remainder in the quotient; we must convert the remainder to the decimal equivalent, in order to post it on the abacus.

To convert the remainder we divide 100 by the divisor then multiply the result by the remainder. The remainder is a fraction of the divisor.

Example:

245 / 6 =

40 x 6 = 240: 245 -240 = 5; so the quotient is 40, remainder 5; or 40 and 5/6: 100/6 = 16.67; 16.67 x 5 = 83.35%

83.35/100 =.8335 rounded to 2 places = .83

Final Quotient is 40.83

On the abacus

245 / 6 =   (6 will go into 24, 4 times and 245, 40 times)

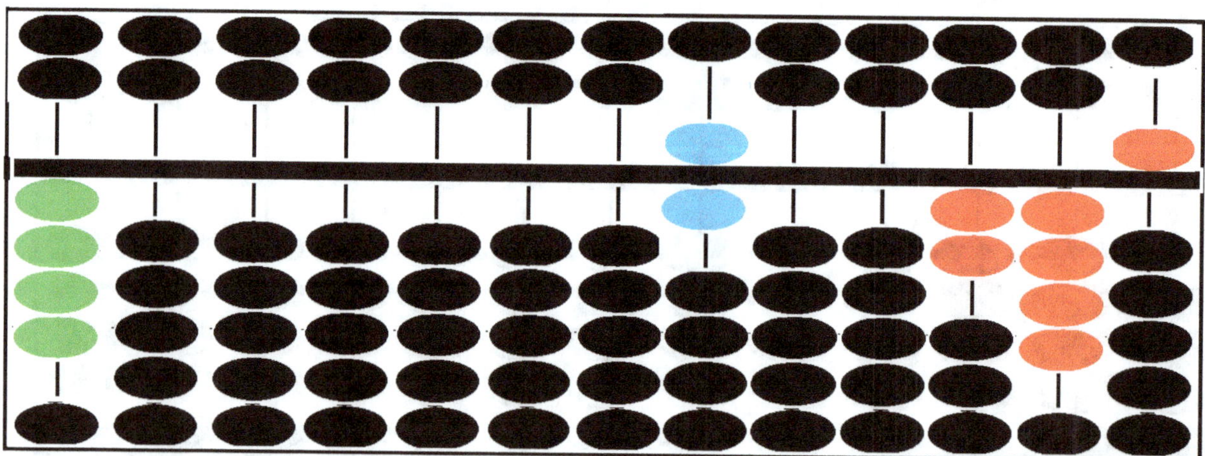

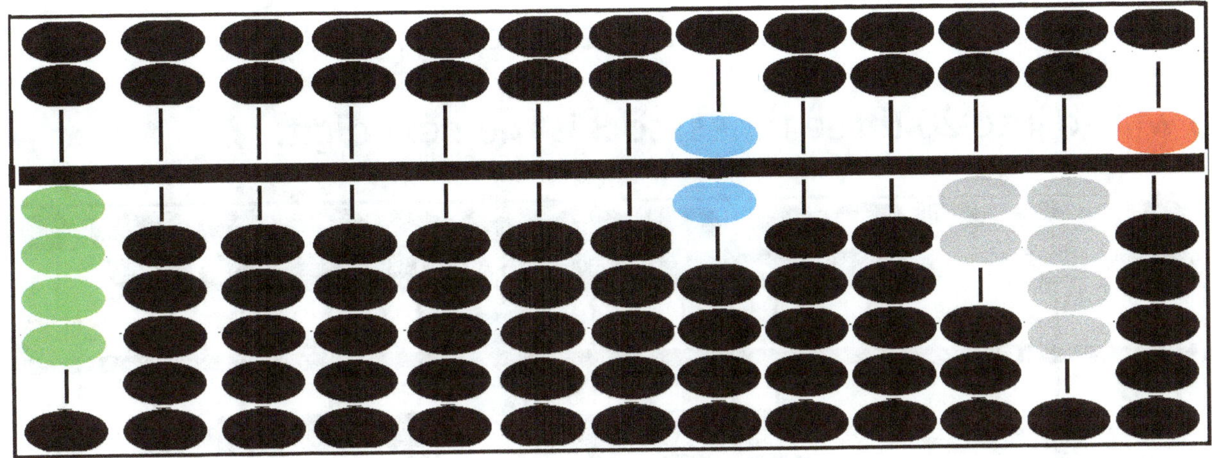

Subtracting the 240, from the left end of the dividend, leaves a remainder of 5. We place a decimal point in the quotient because the remainder will be less than 1; (5/6).

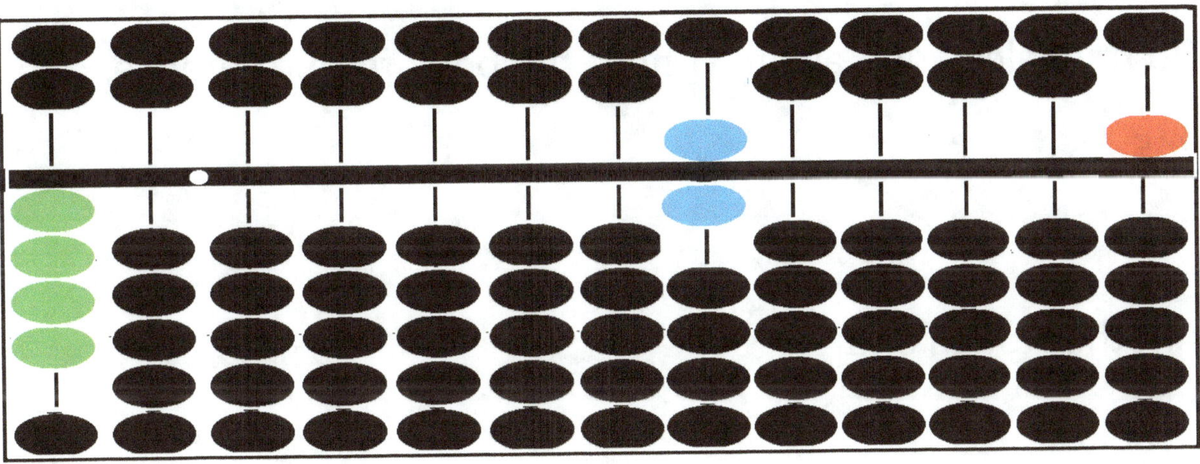

We look at the 5 as 5.0 and know that 6 x 8 = 48, so the next digit in the quotient is 8.

50 − 48 = 2, we make it 2.0 and see that 6 x 3 = 18

6 will go into 20 three times, so 3 is the next digit.

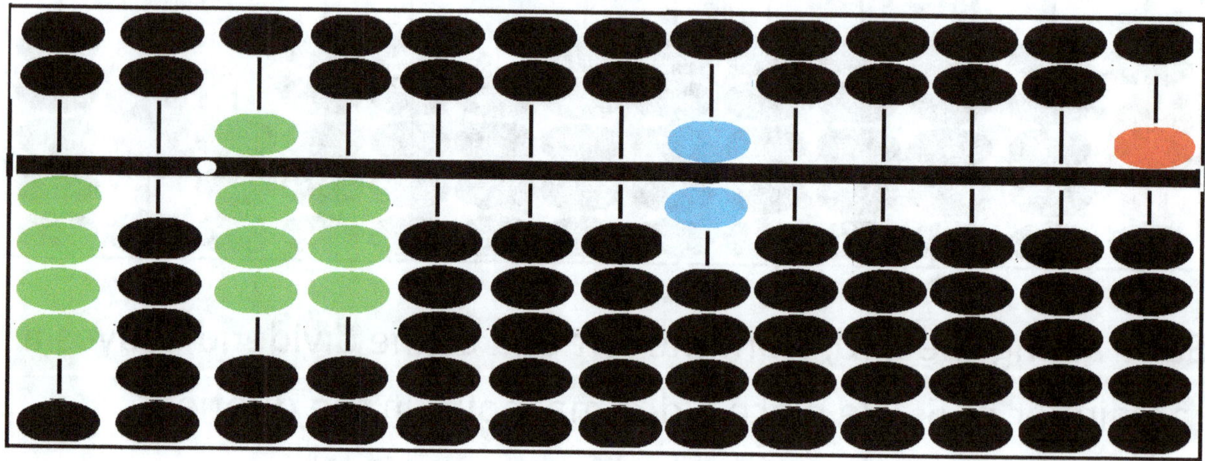

The quotient is 40.83

Do this calculation again without the book for a reference.

245 / 6

Another tough one

1,804 / 23

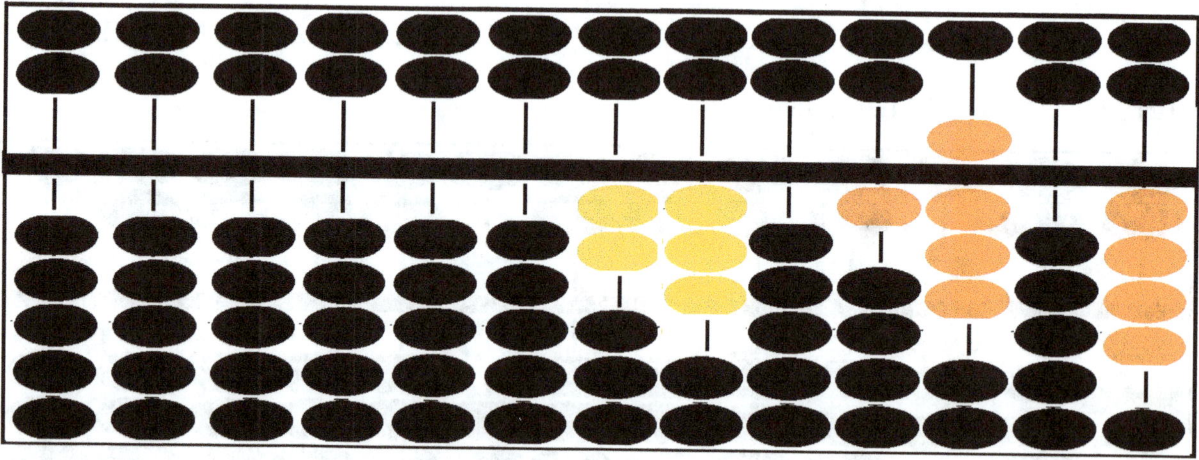

23 is more than the first digit on the left of the dividend; 1.

We next look at the first two digits of the dividend; 1,8.

We continue to examine additional digits until we find a value greater than the divisor.

The first 3 digits on the left are 1, 8, 0; this meets our requirement.

23 will go into 180, 7 times (23 x 7 = 161)

The quotient begins with 7.

180 − 161 = 19

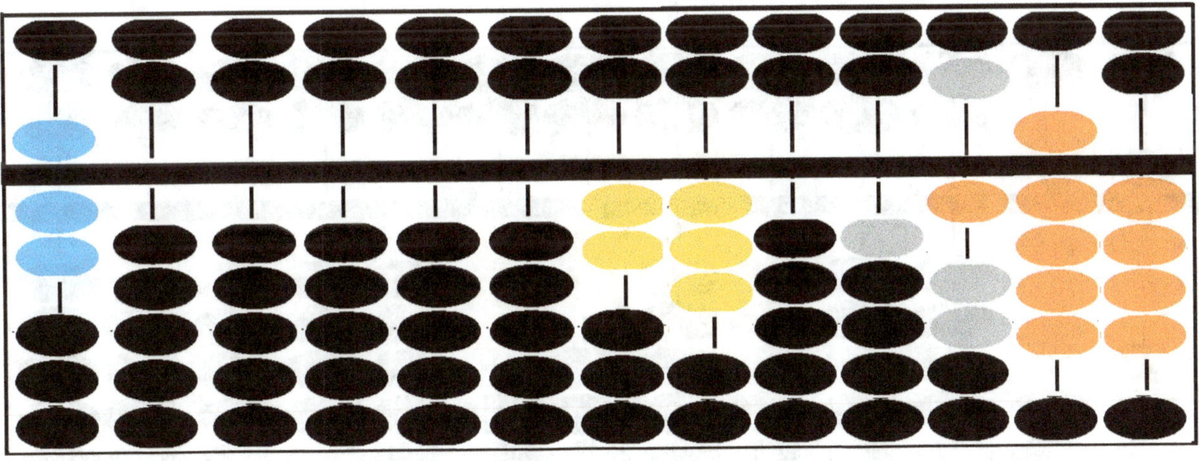

The dividend is now 194 and 23 x 8 = 184

Subtracting 184; we have a remainder of 10.

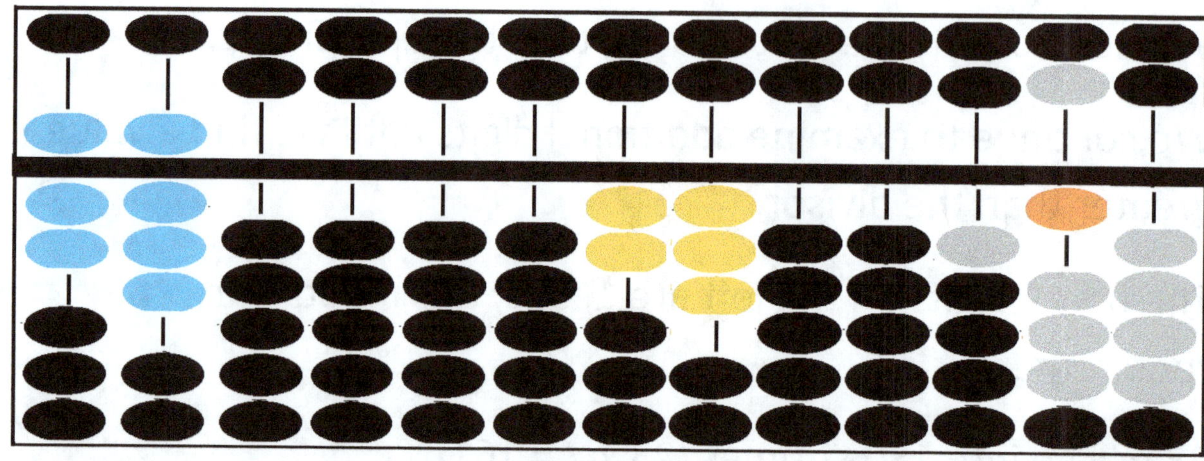

The remainder, 10 / 23, is less than 1, so a decimal point is added to the quotient.

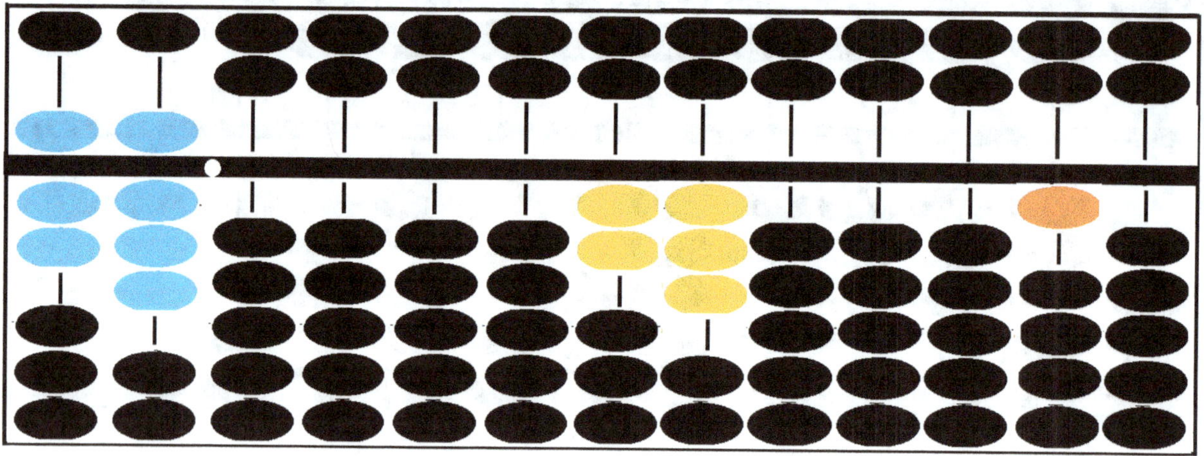

We add a zero and look at the ten as a 100.

23 will go into 100, 4 times therefore; 4 is the next digit in the quotient.

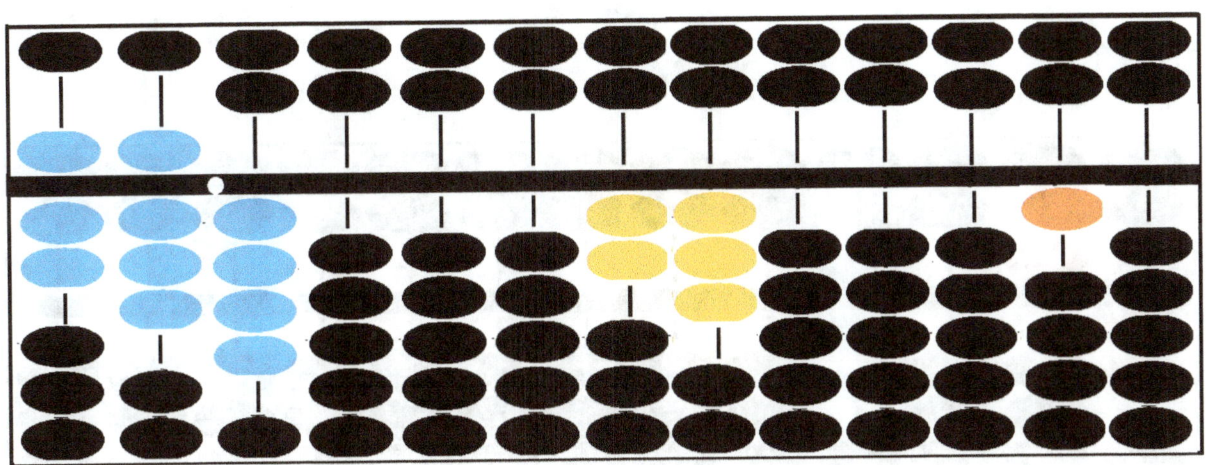

4 x 23 = 92; 100 – 92 = 8; if we add .0 then we try 23 into 80 and get 3, the next digit.

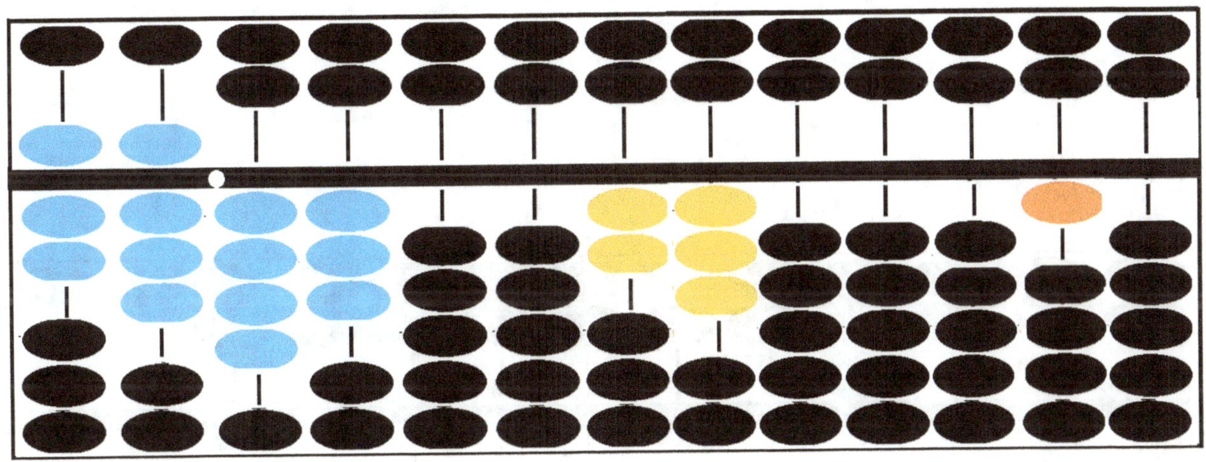

1, 804 / 23 = 78.43

Practice:

248 / 17 =   818/ 12 =   389.4 / 14 =

12,635 / 180 =   7,144 / 24 =   930 / 15 =

Mixed Multiplication and division

(25 x 7) / 5

Step 1

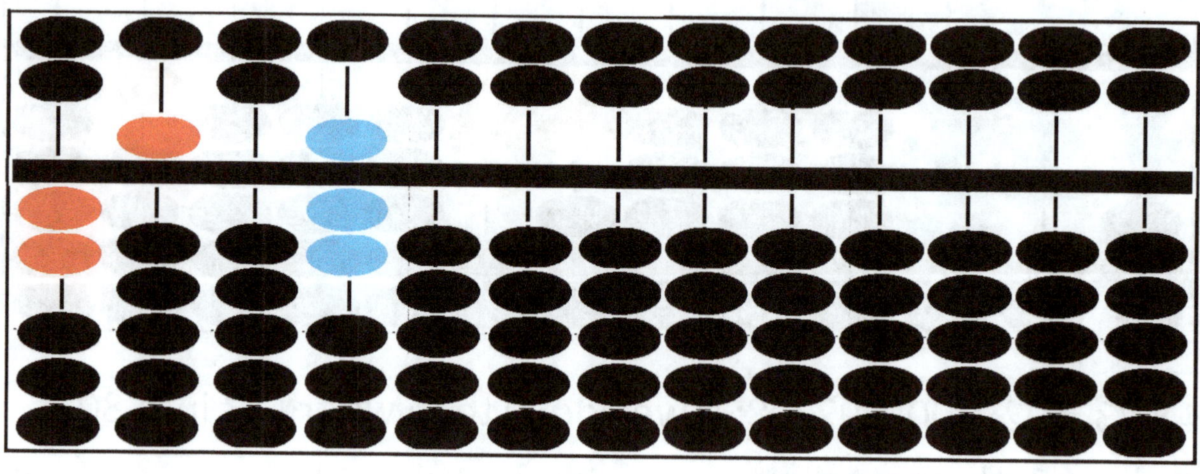

Step 2   25 x 7

Step 3　175 / 5

5 into 17 will go 3 times

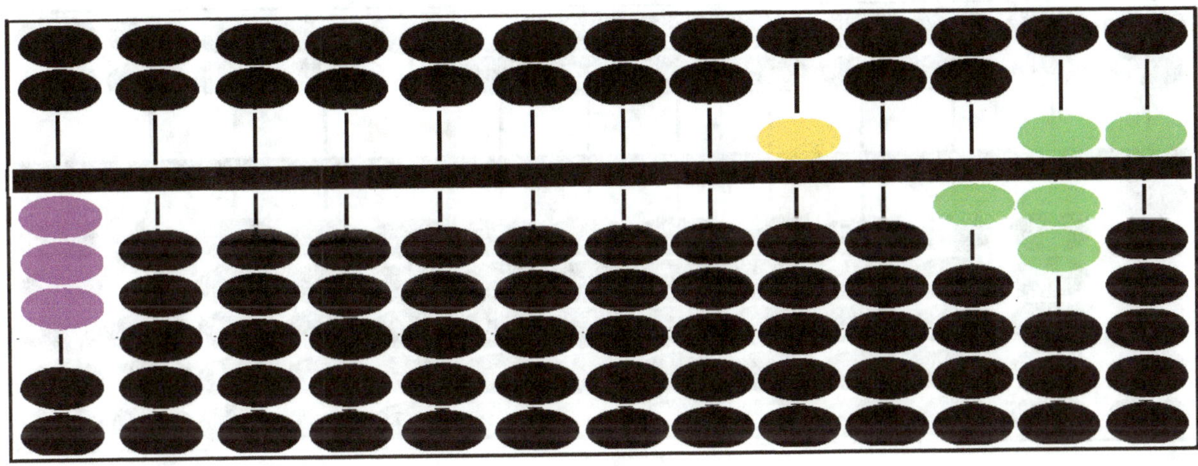

3 x 5 = 15; 17 − 15 =2

5 will go into 25, 5 times; 5 x 5 = 25

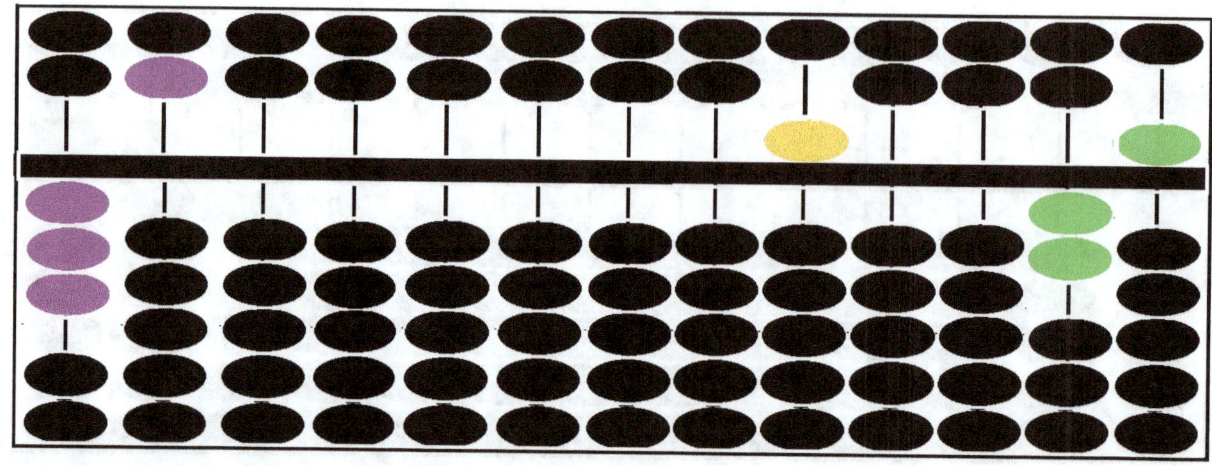

(25 x 7) / 5 = 35

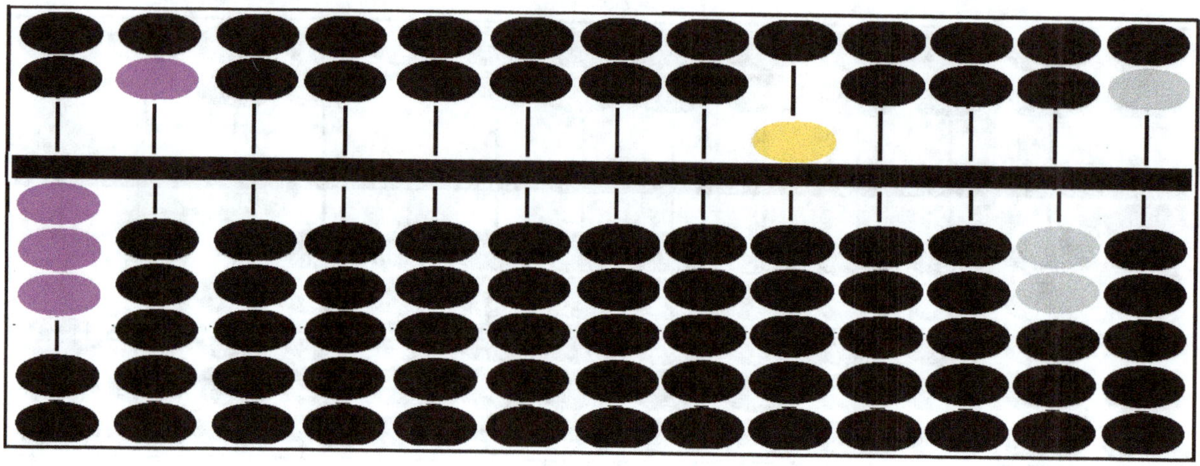

You can leave your product on the abacus and go directly to calculating the quotient, or vise versa.

Practice:

847 x 15 / 42 =

98 x 20 /17 =

387 x 4 / 13 =

22,347 x 14 / 30 =

6,275 x 3 / 9 =

55 x 8 / 100 =

All arithmetic functions mixed

((2+57 x 501) / 293) - 48 + (396 / 4) =

The more you can do with mental math, the less time you will need.

2+57 =59; 59 x 501,

29,559 / 293

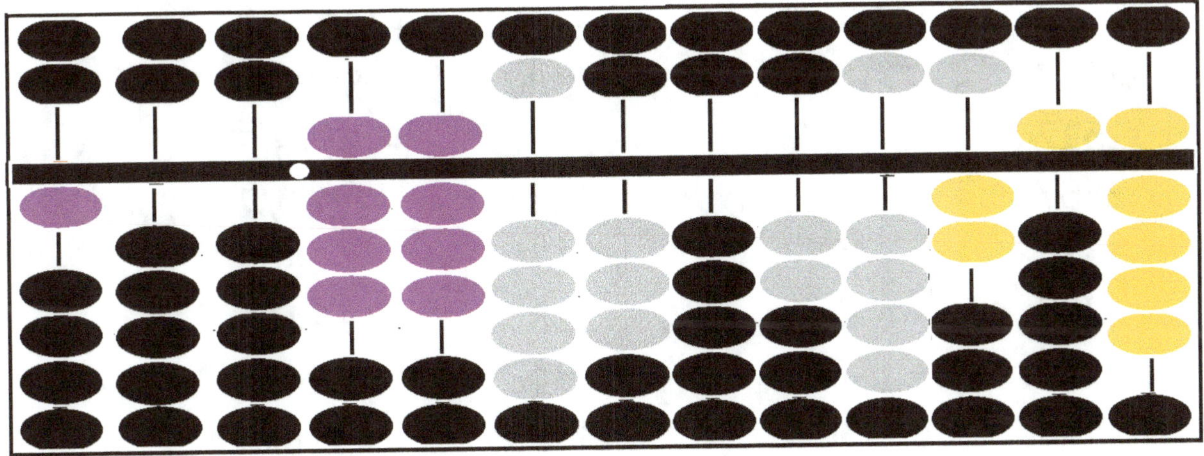

100.88 – 43 = 57.88 + (396 / 4)

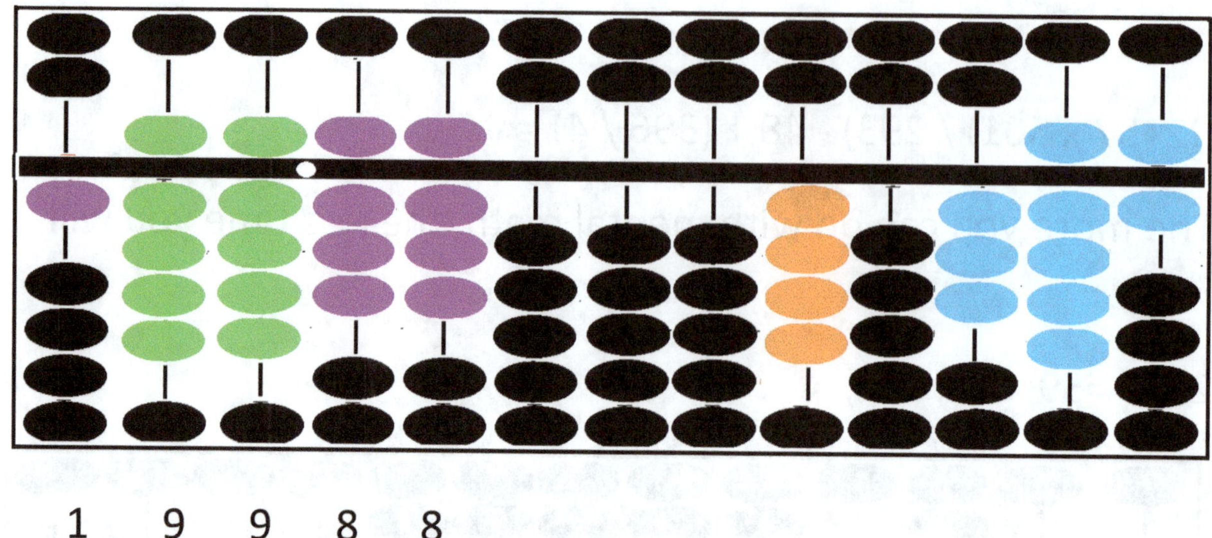

1   9   9   8   8

57.88 + (396 / 4) = 199.88

Try it without the reference: then time yourself as you repeat.

If you are satisfied with your time; try this test.

Goal is 10 minutes or less.

Alpha	Bravo	Charlie	Delta
3417	4741/9	-1875	4180/4
+2790	+1242/5	+279	+2506.38
+2407	-2714x 3	-4980	-3518.09
-1512	+1453/6	+2052	+787x3.5
-2567	+174.25	-3133	-1140/2
+4324	-4023	+1130	-2869
+798	+152x 8	+3989	+2471
-375	-644	-842	-4314/4
+1588	+430.1	+3590	+4318x3
-585	-11.95	-198	-938x1.5

Area

The area (A) of any shape when the measurement around the perimeter (P) is known, is A = (P/4) squared

With your abacus find the area of:

(*Round answers to 2 decimals*)

1) A circus ring, 54 feet around

2) A sand box, 10 x 10 feet

3) A kidney shape swimming pool, 300 feet around

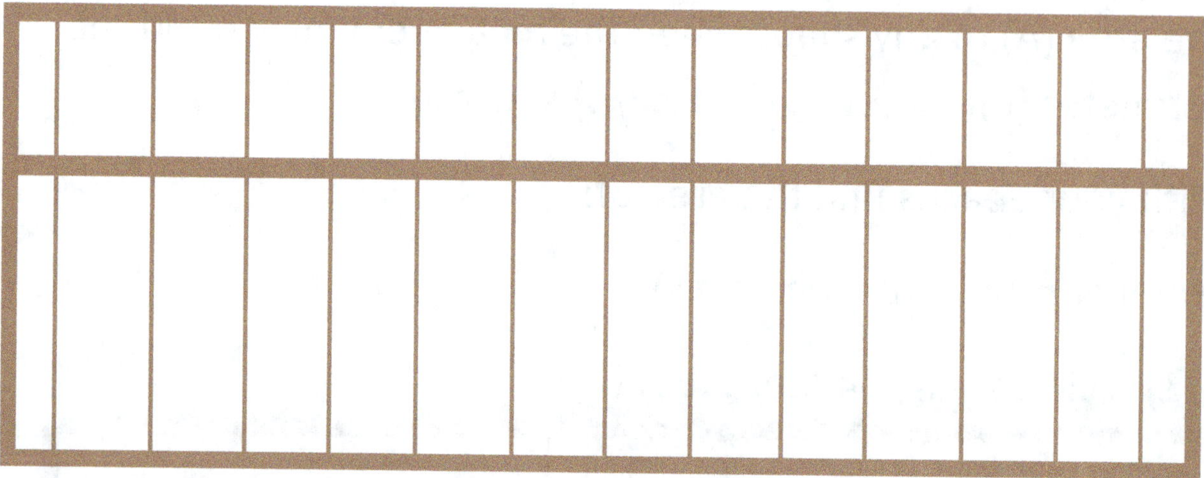

4) A triangle, with sides all measuring 12' 6"

Distance

D = speed x time

At 72.5 mph, how far will a train travel in 7 hours and 25 minutes?

Time

My airplane has been flying for 40 minutes with a headwind of 47 mph, with no wind we will travel 300 miles in 40 minutes.

The time is 2:00 pm our destination is still 1850 miles away

Air travel, D= (speed – headwind) x time

What time will we arrive if the wind stays the same?

Round to hours and minutes

Currency

Harvey bought 305 shares of Slim Bones Dog Food at $45.25 each.

He sold 52 shares at $61.50 each. What are Harvey's earnings from this sale?

George ate lunch at Big Belch because they give him a13% discount. He got the $22.50 special and tipped the server 18%.

How much did George's lunch cost him?

Force caused by acceleration increases by the square of the increase in speed ((new speed / old speed) squared).

We are driving nails with a nail gun that strikes with a force of 25 pounds at a speed of 40 feet per second.

If we get the speed up to 55 feet per second; what will be the striking force of the nail gun?

Objects not filling 100% of a space space

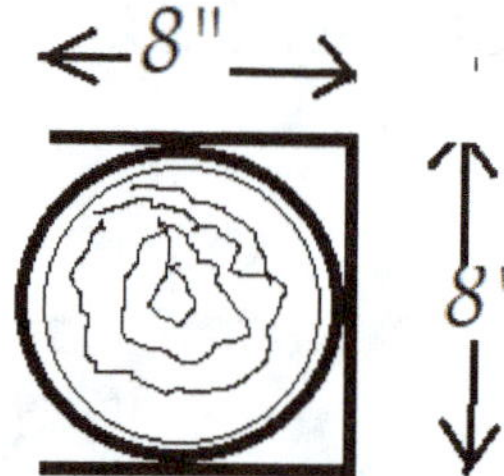

Some round fence posts need to be loaded onto a truck and taken to a ranch site.

The poles are 8 inches in diameter and 6 feet long.

How many poles can be put on a truck, with a bed that measures 7 feet long and 4 feet wide? The height of a legal load may not exceed the width of the truck bed.

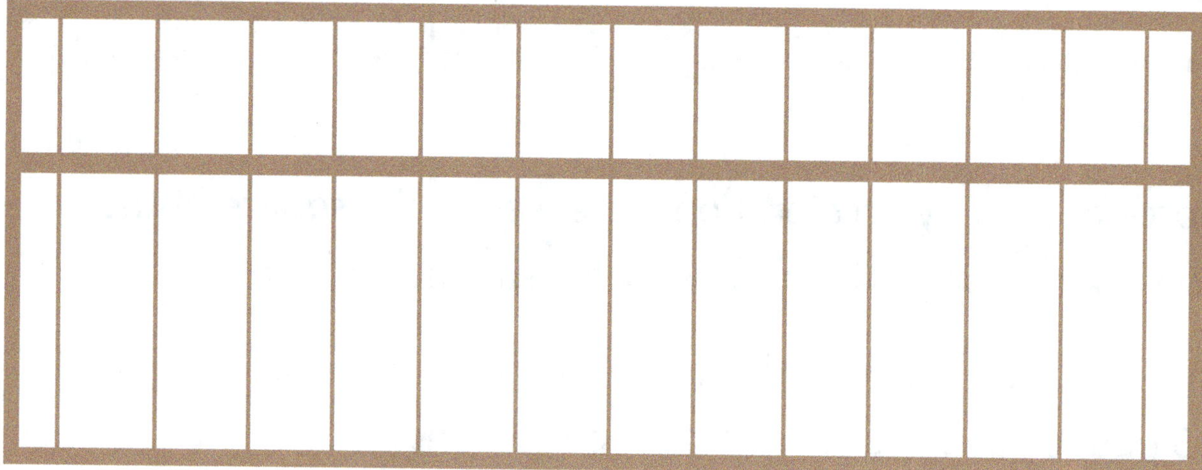

Square Roots

Memorize the squares and roots of 0 through 9.

0 x 0 = 0   1 x 1 = 1   2 x 2 = 4   3 x 3 = 9

4 x 4 = 16   5 x 5 = 25   6 x 6 = 36   7 x 7 = 49

8 x 8 = 64   9 x 9 = 81

Notice the last digit of the squares. Only one ends with 0.

Two end with 1, two end with 4, two end with 6, two end with 9, and one ends with 5.

Find the square root of 208,849

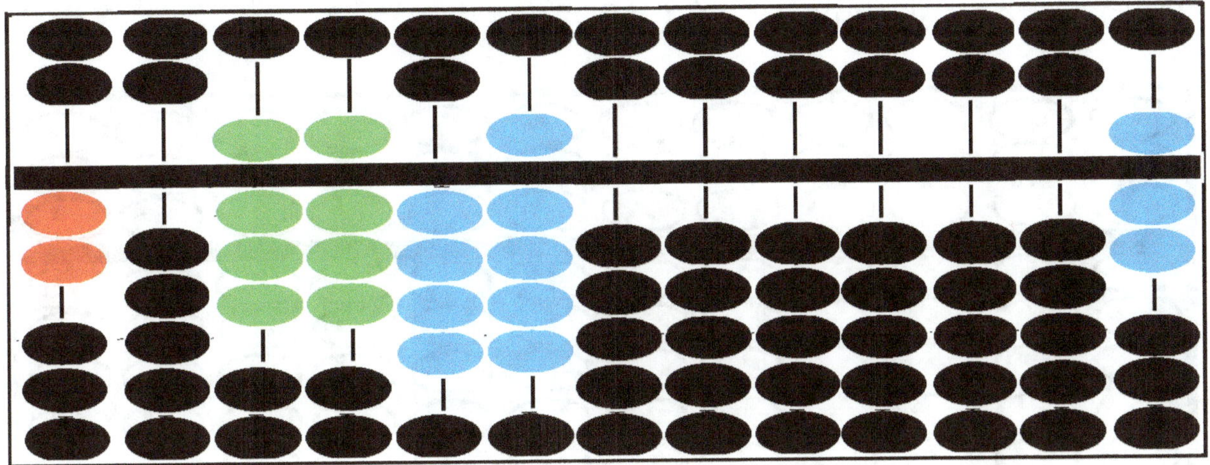

Consider the rightmost digit, we see that the last digit is 9 so the last digit of the root must be **3** or **7**. Now we consider the remaining digits; 2088. We know that 50 x 50 = 2500 and 40x40 = 1600; so the next left 2 digits of the root must be between 40 and 50. We test the halfway value of 45 with 3 appended, 45**3** squared = 205209. We do it again with 7 appended; 45**7** squared = 208849; the root we want is 457.

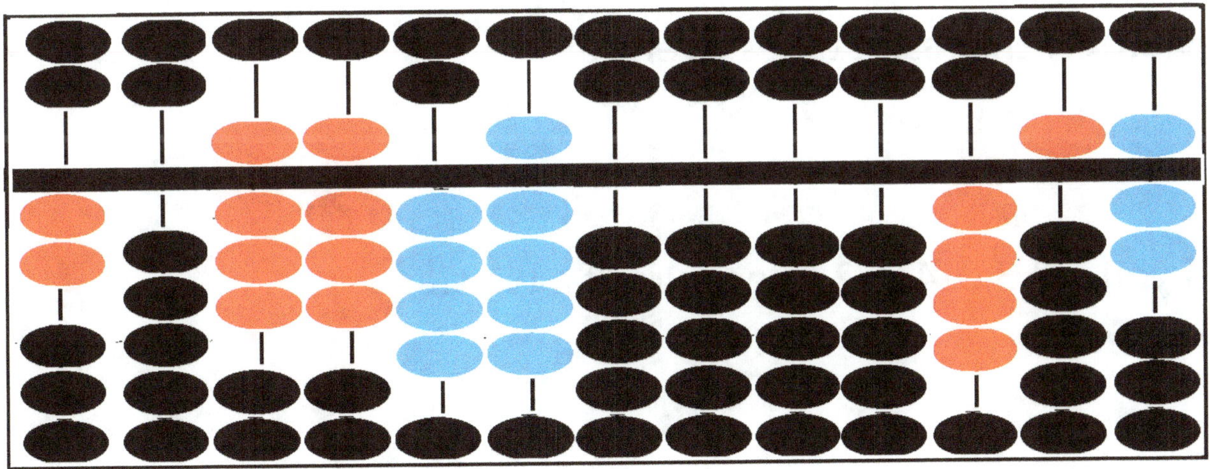

Even though we have little need to calculate square roots in abacus practice; it doesn't hurt to know at least one way.

You may know other methods used to find roots, if so; try them on the abacus.

What is the square root of 1,156?

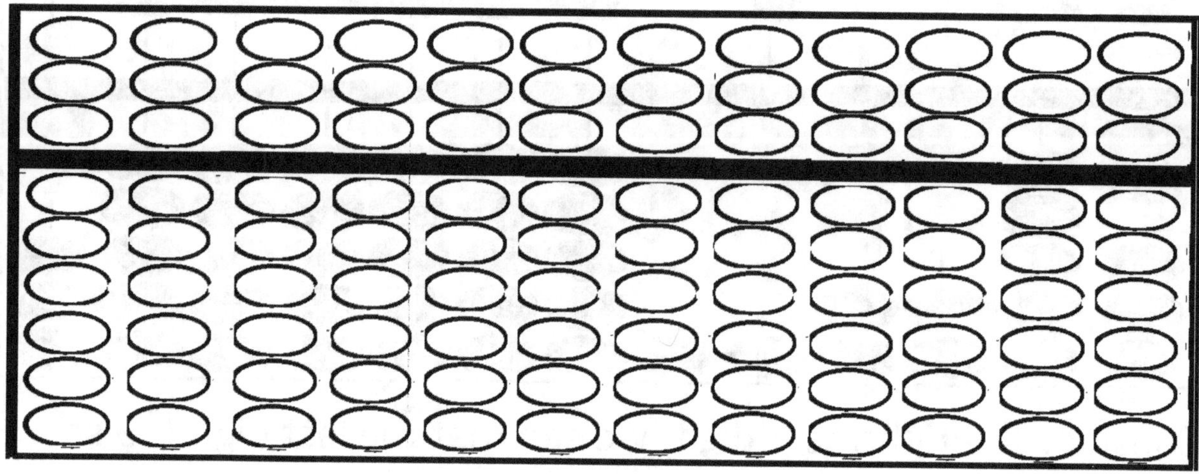

On the abacus, without clearing, in a continuous calculation;
Add 39,462 + 24,184 + 672.801+ 1,930.05

Divide the total by 133.5 and then **Subtract** 245

Multiply the result times twelve.

If you got 3,014.952 give yourself a big star!

4 Digits multiplier

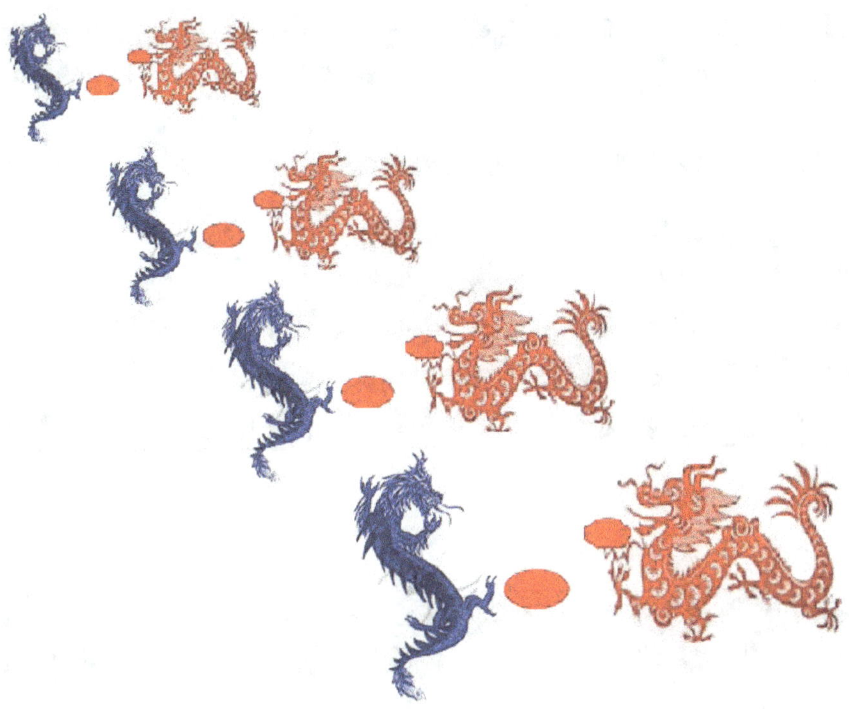

For the last example, multiply with a 4digit multiplier.

380,138.22 x 4,932 =

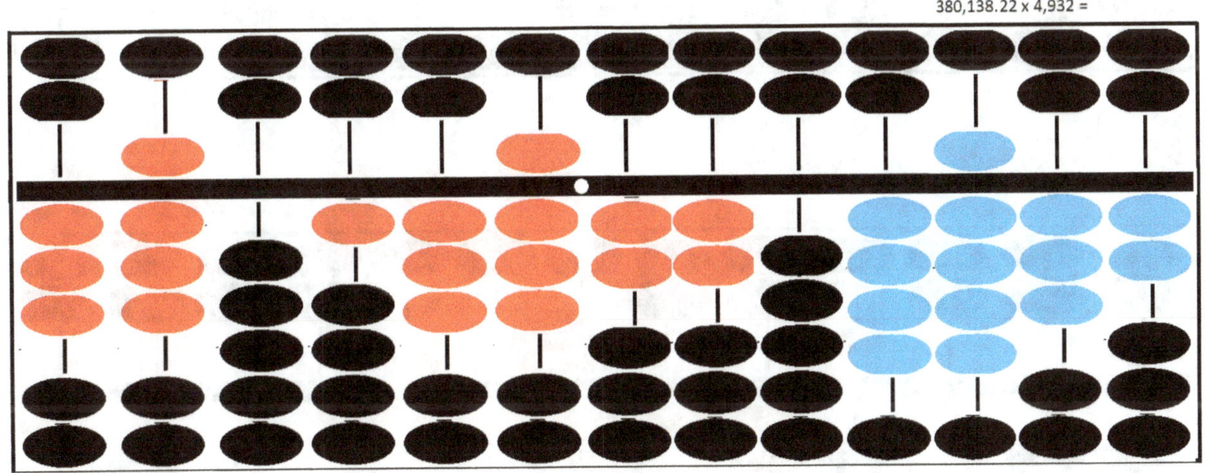

A calculation with this many digits will need more than 13 columns, so we will use another abacus for the product.

Multoplier 2

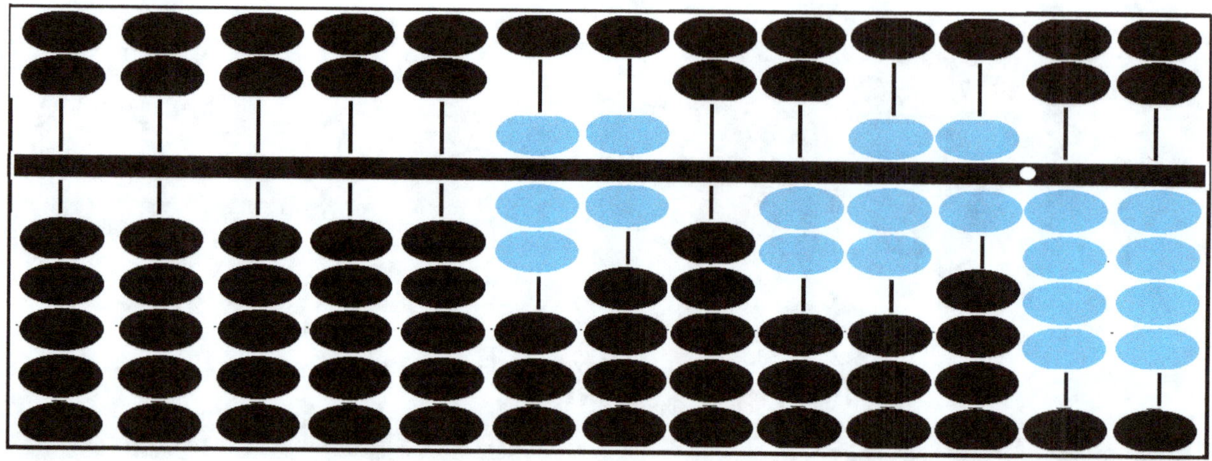

+Multiplier 3

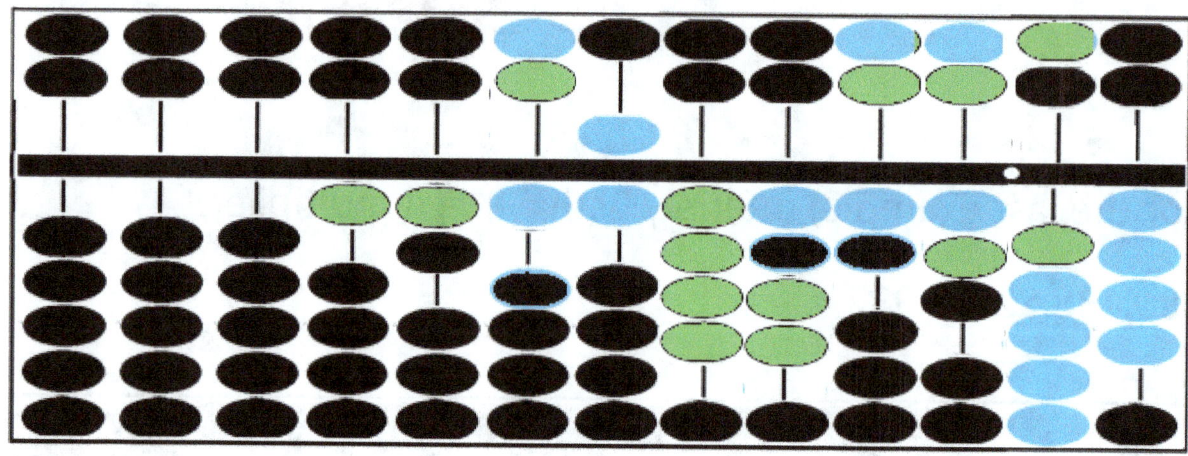

+Multiplier 9

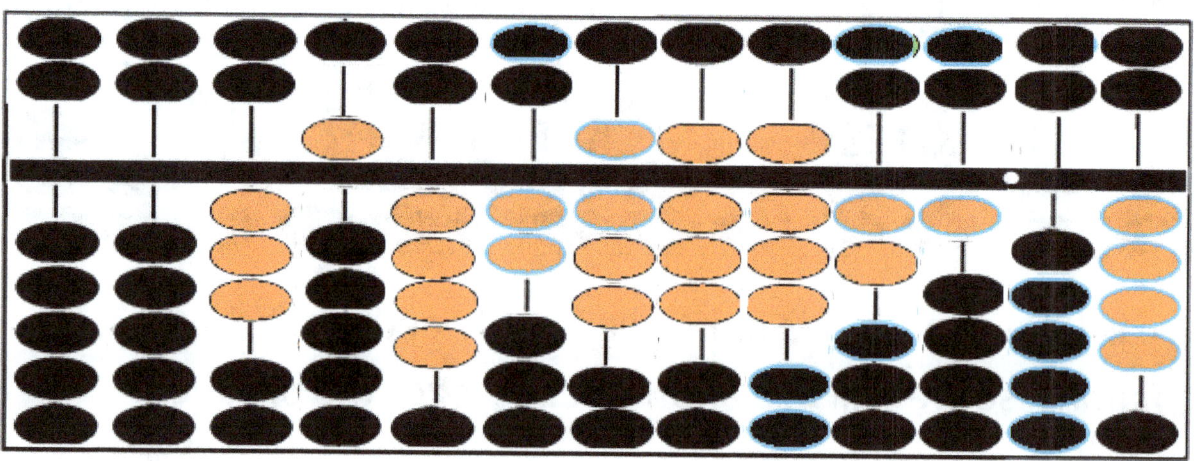

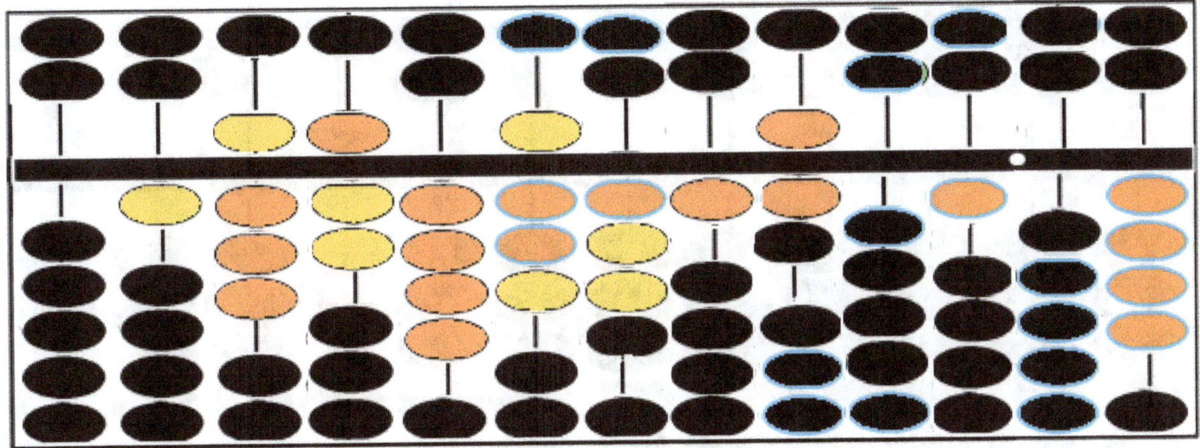

380,138.22 x 4,932 = 1,874,841,701.04

Most Important things to remember:

1. When all five Earth Beads on a column have been used; they must be replaced, at the bar, by a Heaven Bead on the same column.

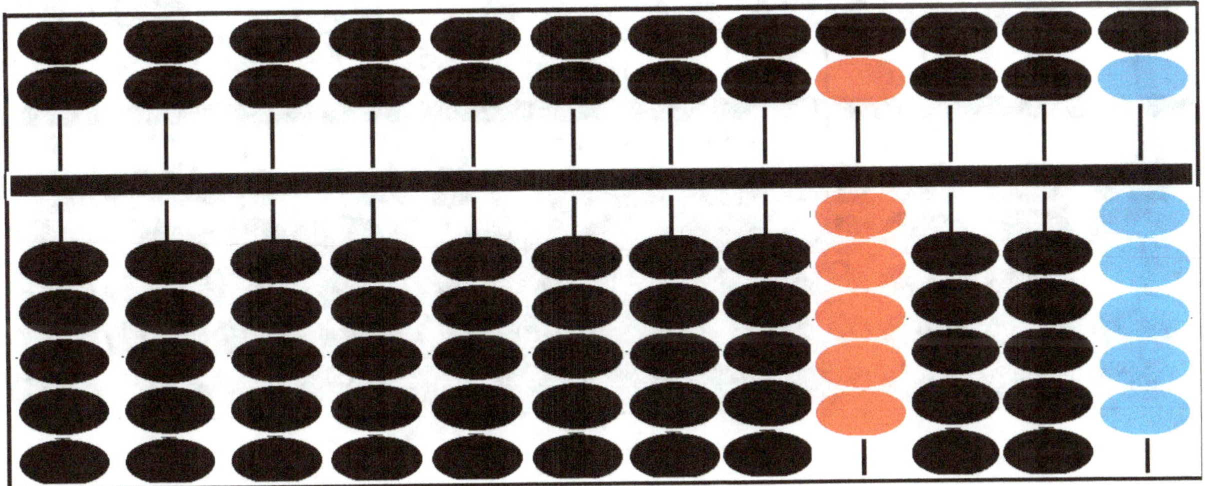

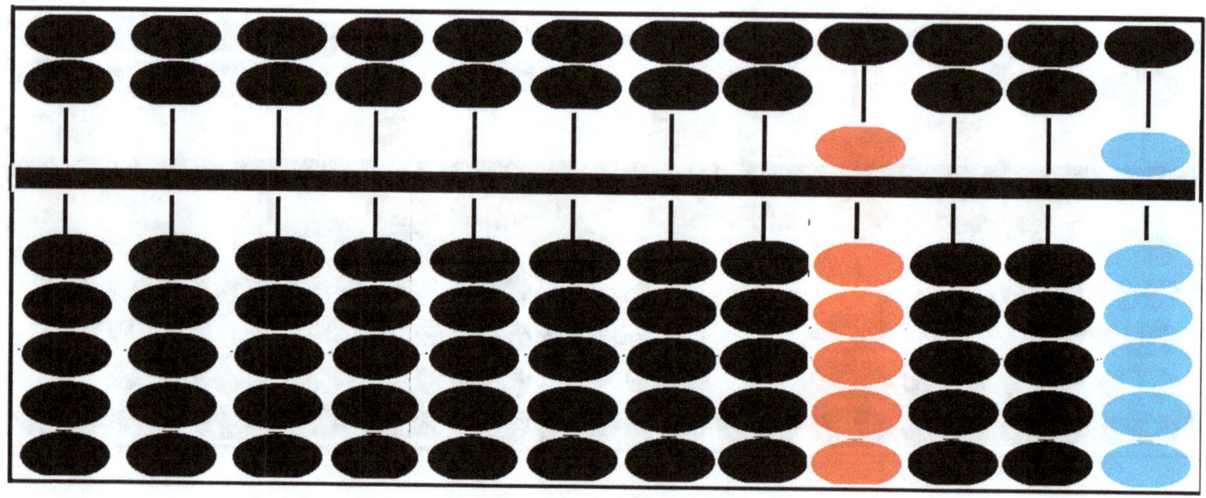

2. When both Heaven Beads on a column are used they must be replaced, at the bar, by an Earth Bead on the next column to the left.

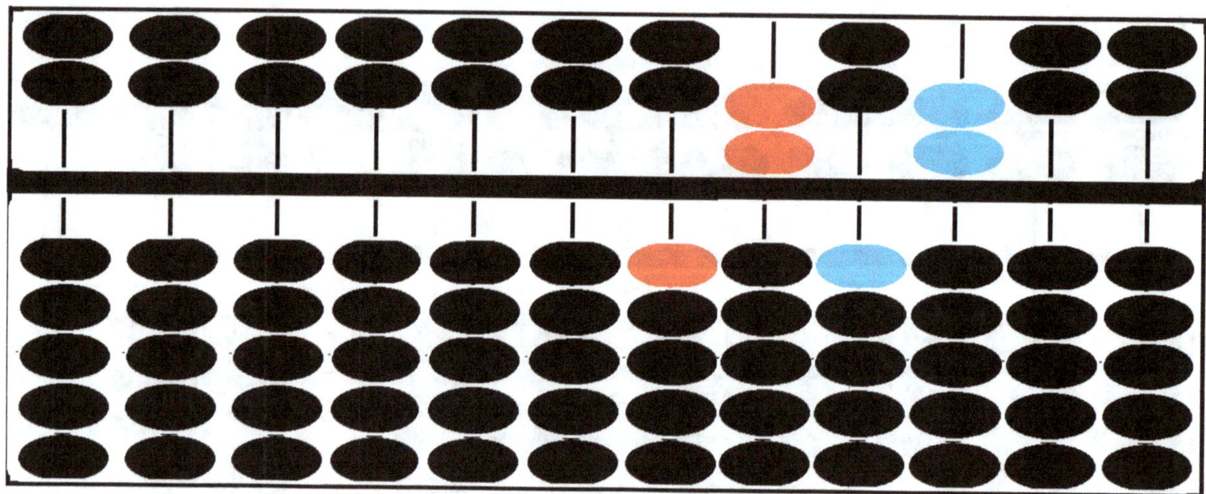

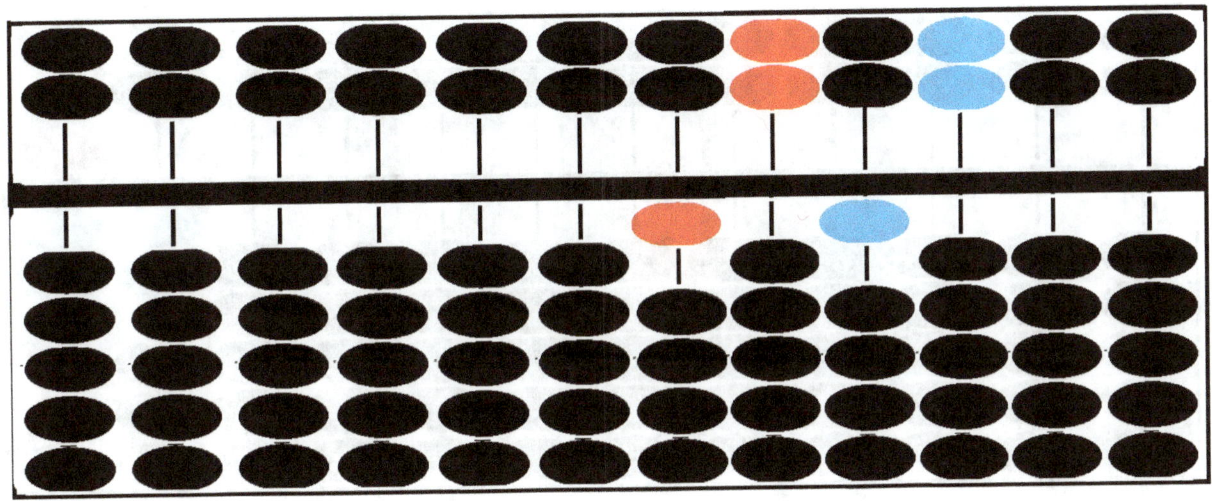

3. When the units to be added are, less than 5, and not available in the Earth Beads on the column, then a Heaven Bead on the column may be added and the excess subtracted.

24 + 3

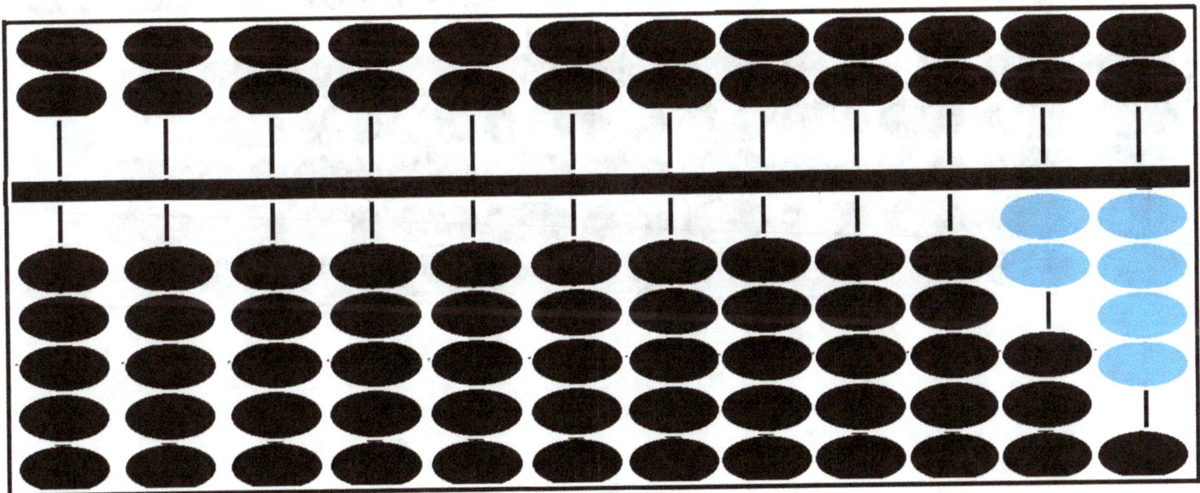

In this example we add 5 and subtract 2

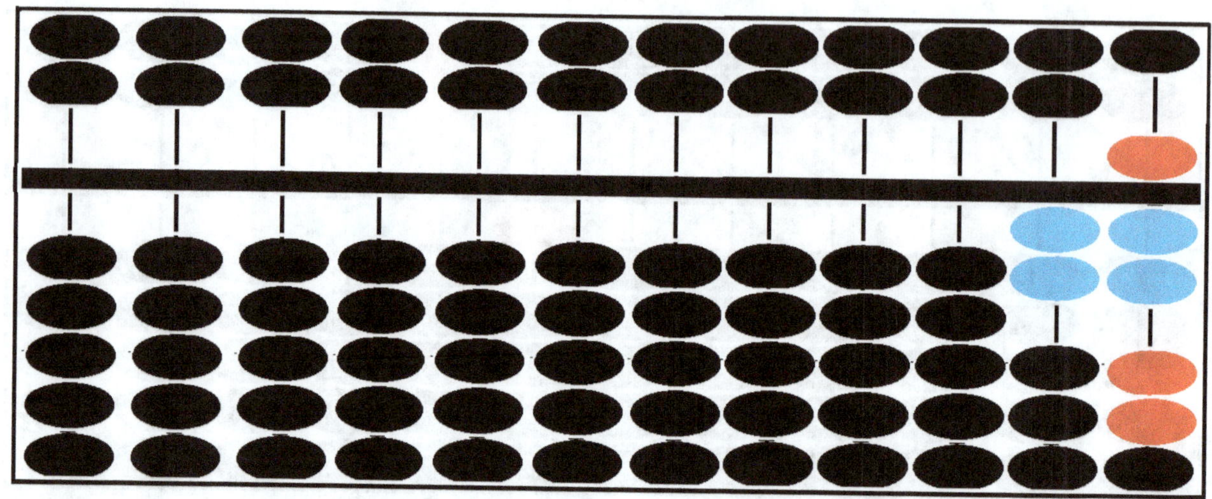

At the bar; 24 + (+5 -2) = 27

4. When units to be added are more than 5 but less than 10; we can add an Earth Bead from the next column left and subtract the excess.

24 + 7

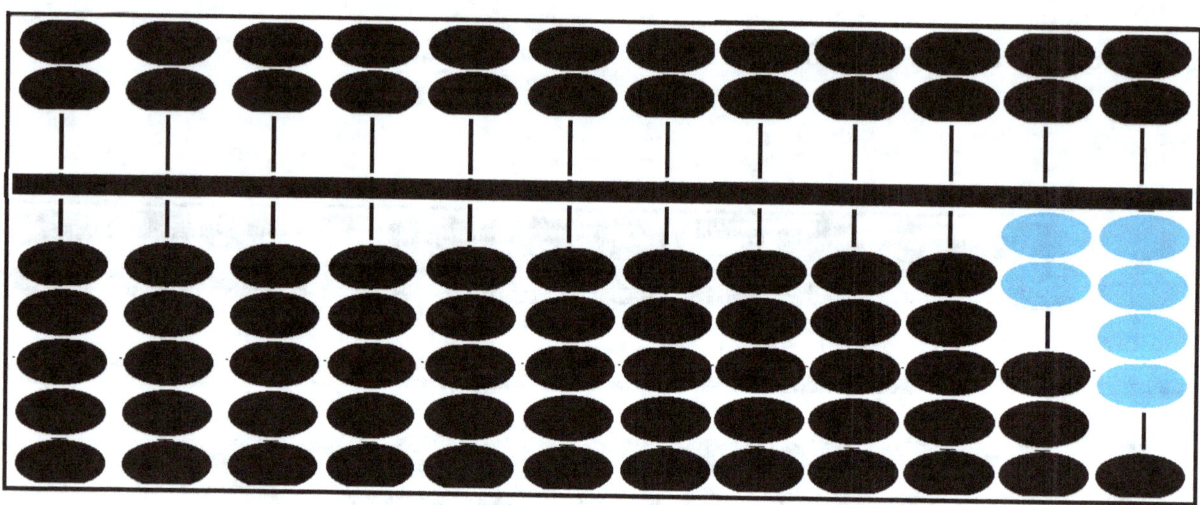

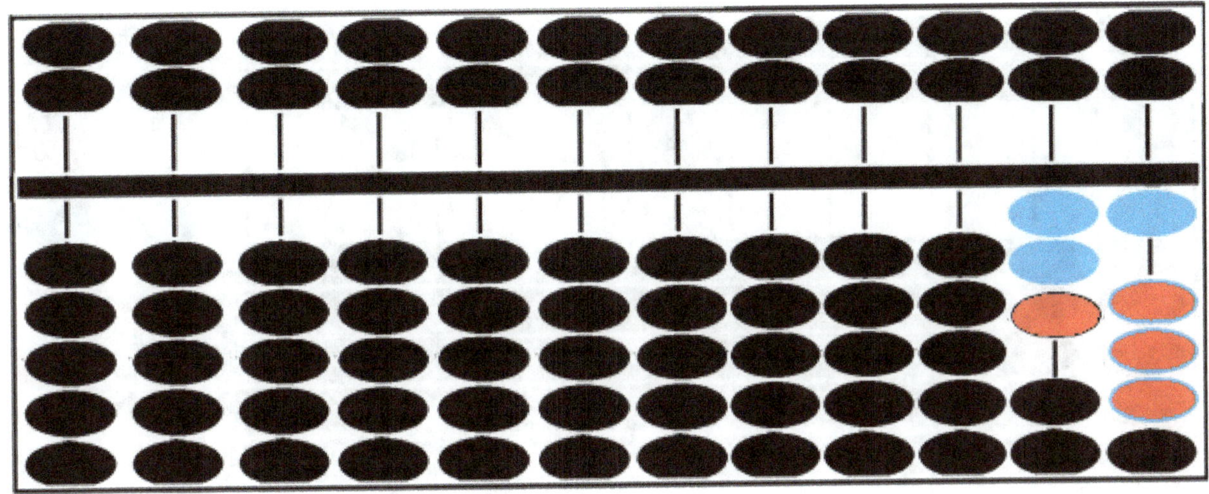

At the bar; 24 + (+10 − 3) = 31

5. When subtracting and the units to be subtracted are not available we subtract a larger amount and add-back the excess.

24 − 8

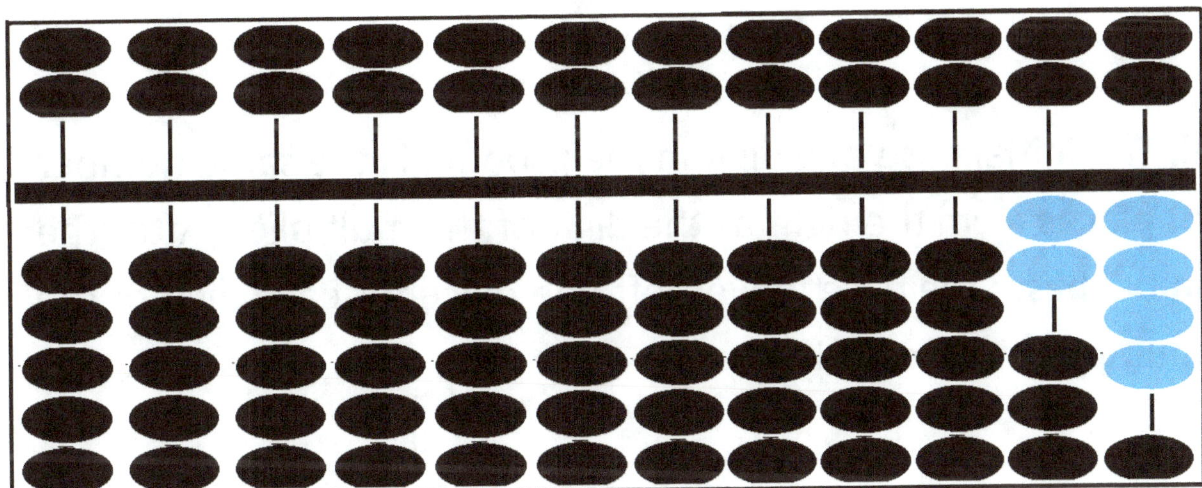

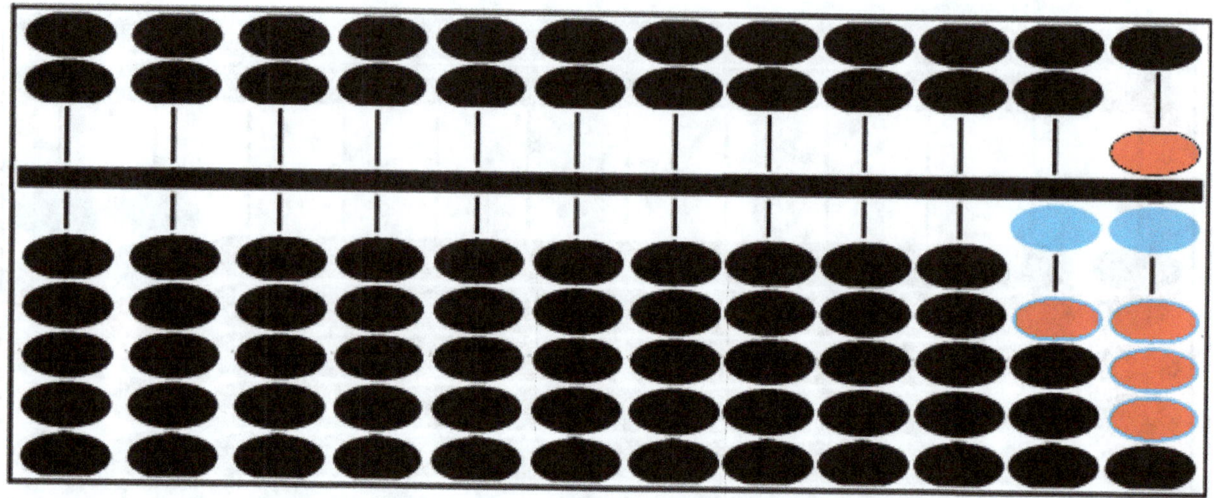

At the bar; 24 – 10 + (5 -3) = 16

6. When multiplying; the product grows from right to left.

7. When dividing; the quotient grows from left to right.

8. The initial base of a digit in the product is the same number of places from the right as the digit of the multiplier. After the initial base; the base moves left one place for each digit of the multiplicand even if it is zero.

9. You decide where the decimal points will be, and it is ok to mark those on the bar or frame.

10. To convert a fraction to a decimal equivalent:

Divide 100 by the denominator and multiply the result by the numerator, the result is a percent. Move the decimal point two places left for the decimal equivalent.

Children able to count to ten on their fingers are ready to learn abacus.

Addition is the usual starting point; then subtraction is learned.

The next subject is working with decimal points.

All of the above must be mastered prior to advancing to multiplication.

Division completes the arithmetic learning; higher levels of mathematics are combinations of all the previous operations.

Joseph W. Salazar

Born Dec. 9, 1940 Chicago Illinois

Enlisted in the U.S. Army at age seventeen, April 1958

Assigned to the Medical Corps and served six years, four of which were in Germany. I worked in many types of Army Medical Clinics and hospitals as a Medical Attendant and Technician. After leaving the Army I lived in Salt Lake City for two years before moving to California and worked as a Vocational Nurse, Driving Instructor, Martial Arts Teacher, and Traffic Violator School Instructor while obtaining my B. S. in Health Science at San Jose State University. I got my J. D. from Saratoga University Law School, Distance Learning Program.

My hobbies are Chess, Martial Arts, Archery and Flying. I also have a Private Pilot license, Ground School Instructor license, and I am a Certified U. S. A. Archery Instructor Trainer. I hold teacher level ranks in Judo, Karate and Jujitsu.

I taught the Accounting Clerk Program for Goodwill Industries for three years and operated my own Tax & Accounting business for forty years. I continue to operate my own business as a Public Accountant.